MUSIC

FOR PORN

MUSIC FOR PORN

ROB HALPERN

NIGHTBOAT BOOKS
CALLICOON, NEW YORK

for Lee

A soldier a real soldier has a worn lace a worn lace.

Gertrude Stein

ENVOI

Having arrived at the end, what I've been dying to write goes on eluding me. This is how friendship assumes its proper shape around all the things I can never say. It's what my mouth wants to be, a hole in the present. To love like this in America is to lose from start to finish. But on our walk up 18th toward Diamond Heights, I finally get around to telling Bruce that I can't bring myself to say goodbye to Mark, I mean forever, as it's pretty clear I'll never see him again, what, with me about to leave for Michigan, and Mark in such decline, and Bruce says I have to try harder, which is the right thing to say, and I know he's right, but it all thickens in my head, crystal grey fog, like in Rimbaud's cities, you know, where men seek distraction under the light they make. My poems don't make more than the dimmest light, certainly not enough to see by. Sometimes it feels like rubbing sticks, and if what I really need to see in order to write what I'm dying to write is the thing the poems so pathetically illuminate, then I think I'd rather see the light go out. Darkness consoles, loosens my bowels, relaxes my impotence, but it can't undo what conditions my vision. I mean, as syntax becomes determinate in the organization of common sense *corrupted love* a whole structure of space goes on eroding at a rate in excess of the time it takes to compose my sentence where I become again the self I've become thru violent contracts. Look how I fortify this grammatical place, ducking into the same dark theater nite after nite, where I'm caught with a soldier's dick in my mouth by a friend responding to yr civil complaint. I'm afraid this is what I've made of my community, anything to claim our ravaged bodies from consuming dark. It all fails to correspond to any sustainable happiness, there being a terminal disjunction between the finished goods and the money available to purchase them. And now, as the rain keeps falling on this deserted town, my social relations cohere around all these militiamen I want to fuck inside abstracted huts where no one lives anymore. So I go on thinking about that walk and about this poem, how it goes on and on and on because the moment to realize it has become my job, my filth, a collective residue, a thin film or integument that hardens around a body interred behind the wall, or buried in the yard, where it goes on secreting the mystery of my well-being. Real intimacy, impersonal as porn. I couldn't even tell you his name, tho a string of phonemes I can't pronounce fills my mouth like his dirty ejaculate, or glue. These words keep me from recognizing him as a person, the proper name being a generic dysfunction that brings us together only to shatter us again. Even the shame I feel is waste. Being nothing more than fealty, this concession to appear if only to dissent for the other guy's pleasure, it's a simple effect of summoning having less to do with ideology than with my allergic response to being tagged, a common ritual triggering disgust, which like rage or ecstasy, were it only better organized, could bring the whole fucking system down. What I mean to say is that it's a risk-adjusted performance, all the bodies yet unburied, failing to coincide with themselves, a scene of permanent displacement, this hygienic bundling, my person, a quotient or lubricant, like liquidity, anything to make the organs useless. Each syllable strung like a bead on a rosary, inserted and teasingly tugged, one at a time, out the hole of my ass. Tickle me here with yr tongue and watch me writhe, the pleasure is excruciating. Like any obsession with what appears self-identical, this sentence binds me in thrall to conspiring forces. Being made of iron and linen, asphalt and glass, my imagination dissembles a soldier's fat, and I get hard just thinking about his hair, completing the circuit of my autopoiesis. Still, there's transport in the body's vegetable existence. Even to have one's name cancelled, stricken from the general roll, demands a witness. Will you be that for me? Resurrection or theft, I'm thinking, as though it were a choice. Many incalculable intervals pass, during which I cling to ghosts of what impossible future haunts the present. Were I to touch the hole in his chest, a spontaneous surge of meaning would suddenly spring to life inside my own incongruent material, the spirit and the beef. Too many voices, can't distinguish my tongue in the mix. In other words, whatever *use* might promise has to begin with its critique, anything to feel the antagonism and not its consensual suppression. This would be the place in the story where Bruce asks me about the figure of the soldier in my book and whether it has some bearing on my intimate life, or whether the soldier's merely an abstraction *is the flesh real?* and I'm struck by his manner of asking, by how his question is just the question Mark would have asked, with the same clarity and concern, uncertainty and skepticism, and I recognize this as being full of implication, both for me and for the writing, even as I formulate my prepared response. Occupier of my inner world, a swan, having escaped its cage on the banks of some uncomely flow, polices my utopian longing like a military mimesis of the mind and expropriates my feelings in whatever way it can. Maybe this is what Oppen means by 'viviparous,' being forever fucked by the thing we're wedged too deep inside to even posit as an object of our own sensation, there being no 'out there' anymore, determinate force having made no mensch of me. What happens, then, when the thing we need to see in order to know ourselves is a corpse withdrawn from view, and when even the language denoting that body has been buried in a classified autopsy report. Being, this spectacular production of absence. But I get off knowing I can at least relate to invisible suffering, lend it some semblance of voice, and then eat the thing of which I sing, filling my depth, feeling common notions stirring, lost in this vessel of exchangeable options. It's always the skin that vanishes first, then what remains, the bone, the ash, and I watch the erosion with perfect equanimity, an effect of everything looking so fucking small up there where we all disappear in larger systems. I heard Verizon is going to refund data charges on my phone, and for a moment I'm feeling sort of happy about that, but if we only could explain the survival of the working day as an accepted unit of economic measure, well, then we might be getting somewhere. As if my poem weren't already yr own blind glass, wedged like a slice of life between the gaping lips of my open cunt. Where ornament shatters, I return the message, listening to the stars for what will never come thru. I mean the soldier, he's my sick muse and deserves more compassion than I appear to offer, but he's already hardened into allegory. Standing in for a blank we can neither fill nor consume, the only thing we share being what isn't here to share, and the promise of that commons. Faking our most sensual relations with wage-slaves around the globe, then harvesting their earnings for warmth. Jerking-off onsite, I imagine a hot day laborer using my shirt to wipe his jizz, then my hand to wipe his ass. Producing appetite thru forced withdrawal, I marvel at the thing's capacity, a magnitude of failing grip. From somewhere deep, waste returns, my constant theme, this decay of sound, a wall of pure significance, the way capital flickers in an Afghani's wound, hedging our implausible intimacies, materializing my love. Identity being at once realized and negated in the soldier I sing of, whatever hope remains remains mediated by the same defiled corpses. Taking note of repetitions, I find myself treading the same terrain. Here comes that stump again, this time sutured to my elbow. As for porn, the fate of bodies constructed by money and the potential disruption of this fantasy. What counts for evidence as the debt ceiling falls on a naked jib. Someone speaks of the collateral necessary to keep the house, driving a wedge twixt life and speech. How my poems drown in murkiness between the twain. Gauged in fabled currencies against the going rate of meat, each new line measured with the spiral of value & profit connects with something deep inside, residue of the old resolve, my mucous, a post-industrial laminate on his cock. Let's lend a name to realer sensations, the feel of finance coursing thru my veins, anything to elevate the nearly unrepresentable limits of the world-system to the level of sense, or to live the positions we already inhabit as the practice of undoing them. There can be nothing more behind what I'm writing, I mean, no one has experienced this event from beginning to end, tho the condition is hardly new. So I've assembled the following discreditable models, jerry-rigged mock-ups of a liquidated tense, negations of abandoned futures, making use of what I can. Rocky lowlands, marginal wood ferns densely covered with golden fur and rarer lichens brought in from the island, bind the world to theologies of labor, all the cotton gins and pharmaceuticals. Upon being hailed, I'm completed by the sudden awareness of my own hideous shape, all feeling dead at the base of my balls. But behind the veneer of these earnest comments lies my excrement and cum, gross product, this residue of debt, cruddy yield thru which we seek transit, a justice in excess of any legible demand. Whereupon I awake with visions of the prison house, abattoirs stationed along peripheral fades, exquisite creatures of social waste, and all the things I'll never see that make me what I am. That's when Bruce reminds me that history is this series of discontinuous shocks connected by the sinewy threads of our own narrations, our friendships and meeting places, but I can't stop thinking about Mark, the way he'd question these poems and how I go on loving him for that.

IMAGINARY POLITICS

— negating the horizon of a totally interpreted world, and our imperiled ways to change it —

THIS PATHOS OF DISTANCE, BEING A THING INSIDE HIM ONCE I FELT

Arriving by night in sleeves to drape the need, coming from somewhere deep inside this absence of birds. The shame in simply being here. Being in my vapors, dim imaginations spooked by cuffs and code, reviving now a tale of rapture, identity withdrawn, murdered, as it were, by the secret heat of combat. Someone's inward hot desire, a lame expression of the need itself, this form, my overproduction. We were once ourselves, but now, traversing the trench, a fault between dim pockets of damaged life, I'm beginning to feel something, a mind without sex, a shudder with no reference, yr breathtaking crevasse, a loss I can't mourn and which I've hastily mapped onto this making of waste. These words extend the body in accord with natural rhythms, and the false immediacy of that. *Exposed before the others* I write, dreaming of belief, crying faith in deadly light. So now there's nothing, the shadow of a name having melted to my cock, their skin, my urethane veneer. The moon, the stars, a spangled heaven nesting deep inside the thing's false pulse, my bald and sunken groin. Our bodies hewn and, feigning being bodies, sundered by forces real. Parts all strewn, my devotional kink, nothing but a likeness, the market's bad effect subliming in a soldier's blood. I wonder what it means not to be here, and then again to be restored. High on all the drippings, steel pressed thru and rubble heaps, self-preservation bearing fond and sensuous relations to all the circuits of exchange. No sound of war reaches an ear. Who could be tracking it, sensing arms flowing partial objects — population, some sick incomprehension or technique — now become my own unsavory implants. Fat preserves the subject through all this. Procedure takes the place of each intended fuck, a model for fresh trade. The ordinance, being one such cited custom, why won't anyone oppose it *and woe that anyone is me*. Of the dropsy, the surge, we had foreknowledge, but I made no provision against it. A measure of the world's duration, our meanings either dissipate or gel. Once there was the sun, but even that's untrue now. Trying to restore some semblance of its lost remove, making brave contact with my absentee. I'm afraid not a single one of the military age males will be interested in seeing my hard-on. Having flushed subtracted figures with bleach-related products, human tolls arrive in even more accommodating terms, like those of the vehicle and its plush interior. I've counted one truly achieved identity and its shape resembles nothing of my flesh. Can't we just release ourselves from this incomprehensible work, slough it off, I mean *workers of the world, relax!* That's what my fifteen year old hustler said — terrorist, nigger, thug — before they discovered him dead with an even more disreputable man several months later. Examining my experience, safety gleaned from market share. What's become of their organs *all scenario, no plot* and why doesn't yr blood rush thru my veins. Disinterring utopian scenes like this one, it all contracts a rather brackish taste I've grown to love, as if waste were the incalculable thing itself, our promised frontier. Siphoning fuel from sewage, unwinding into national moods, looting all the shit our forms so endlessly incorporate, nursing on withdrawn spectacular slaughter. Now undo this habit. The park's replete with room, a widening fault negating the future as mere extension of the present. This won't take long and we'll emerge, together, a hole blast thru the audio feed, our ears, at last prepared to hear, discovered in the mud.

THIS EVOLVE, BEARING NO RESEMBLANCE TO LOVE

having come from the forest, forgotten place of cardboard and gum. our deciduous means, a verdant slick, anything to free my sentence from this obsession with waste. you no longer being, my abundance, a blank the world keeps repeating. such pure situation, miming a death i can't mourn. *and y're not even hard* you say, meaning me, my unforgiving visibility, the repetition and the sentence, a heat seeking form of command gone cold forest trees without birds, rain. this unlivable passion, being what engenders me. and sexless still, yr foot in my mouth, yr face a smear across my chest, a slow drip down the throat. now turn that feeling into something mathematical, dynamic, you say, or is that me begging them to bomb. y're the barn wood, the clover, a figure of vast duration, cuneiform or moss, the equal of silurian mounds, a system of great rocks progenitor of my turnip, my fern. were the record to appear preserved intact (no blank, no skip) there'd be no way to know if something really happened. being the site of subtracted possibility, a trace of real currency, sign of absolute exchange, one little hole. *and y're not even hard* you say when down on my knees, exposed before the others, unbearable repetition, a piece of mortar shell, a bone. history's limit, my lost marine yr role in something boundless makes me impotent, a blank the war keeps repeating, a bad infinity gone sublime. you come from the land of ur, forgotten zone of oil and steel. these things extend the body, my operations of regulatory power. kissing barn wood, rubbing rock, yr clover grows over everything. it all fades out beyond the true, my one unwritten sentence, this forest of dying birds. would that you were only meat having contracted yr absence, this is of the purest sound. repeatable whimpers, skips in the record, my unforgiving audibility. a thing i'll never hear arouses me, begging you to enter the objects i'm investigating. his hair. his wood. his barn. his clover. relics of my rapture, birds remain outside my sentence. you say, i don't believe a thing you write. i say, i don't remember myself, it could have been anyone something in the mind gone cold. take the turnip, take the fern. the rock. the sun. the wood. the meat. would these things be true without that body's résumé of torture: *sunken eyes, the ears taped back, the nails pulled out, yr tongue, perhaps it's mine.* y're all commanding skin, a repetition having not yet achieved the status of event, or being the absence of that. a pure excrescence, abundance itself, a small thing seeking heat y're already something else, a body swollen, flecked with fern. the wood's immense, the clover shines, the barn, a darkened globe. all things equal here, exchanging you for this or that, silurian mound, great system of rock, a turnip, the sun. being my land, you said, cluster munitions, combat heat, the sediment and foam. a thing in the mind now gone. take the ammo, take the birds. my body, being anyone's, a blank repeating his already dark season of migration, deciduous and hard, looming in a cool inebriate sleep. having come from beyond the bay, the barn, the rocks, the moss, the clover. my abundance, being you no longer being. i remember a likeness so exactly, the way you came, my spectacle of duration, something inconsolable, bloodless. like wood from the forest, our moment of pure arousal, this being in my sentence, or something standing in for that, the war the forest and the rain, yr face, my verdant slick. nothing resembles, nothing to see, an abundance without birds. erection and machinery, no tongue on my thigh, the world that made you possible, gone now, too. i feel dirty. my soldier running, or my image for that, a corruption in the record. such clean subordination. broken subjects, surface areas and coastlines now contiguous with the vastness of that blank, repeating what won't go down *and y're not even hard* an imperfection in my sentence, a timeless skip. excitement reigns, the heat of combat, a swollen digit up my ass, a forest, now a park. no kiss so sweet, no rock, no sun, still miming a death i can't mourn. duration reduced to mortar shell and bone, and the value of this communication measured by that. you, being nothing now, my every impression, a land once separated, now joined by meat and mud   .

THE TOWERS AS ARCHITECTURE

Now a few words for my Christian Zionist friends. Fuck me with
the things our meanings make. The IMF or an AK-47, my purest
intermediaries, a surplus of dead. Love, being a model for the war,
you can be a hole in the present, a real event, but *I am the towers!* as
architecture wipes out the commons. Please take that burqa off. This
is about belts of pink broken by all the tumbling barns, accidental
sanctuaries for migrants and wolves, where endangered birds speak
only to foreigners as they prepare to traverse the trench. Like the
UN, poetry can't appear to take sides. Money being a species of
protected speech, the world's a thing that isn't here. Turned back
at the line between 'free zone' and 'siege,' unaligned forces call for
appeasement, but that was under Clinton, when state sponsored
humanitarian aid was better prepared to dissemble my interest. Time
appears as tho it were a thing we didn't make, measured in square
feet of old suburban junkspace, our nearest collective negation. So
I've put a harness on the object to mask inhuman features. A class
of idle bondholders perk up my private flows, a direct intervention
of providence. Thus we begin our trek across the zoned terrain, the
lawns and acres paved, bodies we once called our own, setting out
toward new illegible structures rising in the East. The idea is to clear
the park of all the faggots and whores who masquerade as menace.
That's when a handsome young soldier whispers something dirty in

my ear — *techniki techniki* — a fossil of my own deep sleep. Having nearly lost consciousness, like common sense, I feel so immaterial. Buried in the dream's withdrawn terrain, we mistake our fucking for a truth procedure. I, being a thing subtracted from what inner life obtains, this convergence of lyric and ballistics, my urge to dispossess and own. That's when I come like a font of glue, publicly transported in the impugned space between the last outhouse and that skinny neck of disputed land where crisis grafts my sentence to a blown-off limb or stump. What if we really do end up somewhere, he asks, pressing my head to his thigh, touching me where I'll never count as one, arousing all these gestures of defiance no sooner made than recuperated by surplus buying power and its impress on my poem. Permanent disabilities absorbed by the system, cushioned by all the promotional brochures that insulate and kindle. What might it mean for this plot to develop. Having arrived at junk status myself, declassed by overproduction. It's easier to understand the thing's dissonant structure when you hold it at some distance for better reception. You can even use my lips to create a deep syllabic hush, being the likeness in time our fulfillment inflates. Who's not terrified of being left alone in that aloneness with only a screen to drape the dirty thing my leg keeps doing and upon which I see myself projected, impersonal remains of consequence, a blank expanse, my mouth moving in sync with yrs as you read. So many of my old memories disgust me. A blowjob in the boy's room determines my capacity for military use. You can come inside my free trade zone without protection, I said, and immediately felt like a dope. I'm a huge concrete flower, a long list of dead ones. Just make me yr allegory for *soft penetration of the East*. I can be yr restive subject population, a friendlier investment climate, begging for water and morphine. No one's thinking about what Mao said now, and the E on the stone's an empty sign. Who cares when it's another free morning in Tahrir or Liberty. I mean, I love you with that air of Jacobinism and leather *wool hide meat oil fat* contracting air-conditioned tents and morticians to service the finer sinews of engagement. But there inevitably comes a moment when you ask yrself, how many days will I be here?, and you divide that number by the amount of money it takes to buy the place, and I guess that's the difference between being at home and being in Gaza, Fallujah, or Beirut. I admit, it was pretty amazing to see them fall down, but I've since lost all feeling below the waist. 'And in their destruction the thing stands stronger than ever as a living symbol and a certain promise,' said Benito Mussolini, circa 1932, regarding the removal of the Venetian lion from the town loggia in Trogir, Croatia, which had become a State possession in that year. Now we're working undercover as incendiary pacification and growth, writing something history can't write about itself. No origin obtains in the forms we create, but when we emerge from the mud we all have names.

SOME SPECULATIONS AROUND GEORGE OPPEN'S PAROUSIA

— not being altogether opposed to crimes of violence —

— "the casual horror of the iron"

(By which he must have meant being

Penetrated by some impenetrable thing I
Mean fucked & nailed to wood a beam
Still singing of sky or stone or glass

Anything to name and so by naming
Make the thing appear to overcome
Its own idea or the labor that makes it

Look unimaginable a gleam so hardened
By time a speech so impure so perfectly
Coinciding with the nail my thing avoids

   — *yr emptiness impossible to bear.*

•

Like boys birds leave no hope
For anyone to sing or say all this
Isn't real it can't be happening

Such certainties of doubt we have
Fashioned ourselves out of things
Penetrate me like the nail does

Wood the skin secures its ~~rupt~~
Raptures verities time being full

— of what we've failed to make.

•

We fucked up when we woke up to them
All reaching for us not noticing ourselves
Being in the way not being here to reach

Out far enough to touch our own survival
Old horizons a whole new nature leaping
In stone labor a glamorous distance closing

In closer than yr fucking plasma farther than
The farthest stars engender sense in common
Places so grave a report these paths appear

         — more than 'arduous.'

•

Being the hidden starry life our language hides
What it can like any body would and dreams
A politics as if whose history has no future

Perfect losses we can't mourn what we have
Erected structures voiding space things that will
Have come inside no place being where we live

A fantasy of home secures their missing limbs
My cock ensures them tender organs fulfilling
Orders of state when they migrate with no bodies

And even more flexible forms

— *this 'achievement of the housed.'*

•

So this must be the passion whose
Patient parousia by which I think
He means a body in a present

One's own

        — labor failed to make.

•

To say that something's close say
Sky when only you can cancel
My disbelief [——] says the nail

Will never touch this nail the sky
No longer being sky yr bone
May never be my bone not being

Dead conviction in what's not here
Has won my luxury to doubt
The material from the material itself

Such caesurae to inhabit a blank
Expanse a kind of consciousness
Entitled to disbelieve this eros a ruse

— being the very structure of my thought.

•

— all this acquires an appearance

Of what simply exists as feelings they've been given
To mysteries penetrate me because loss is so fucking
Productive and the everyday restores it all to the side

- real labor ~~embodies~~ enjoys more of my impenetrable
Shit having migrated from vaster reaches imagin
- aries meaning matter things we didn't make this

History being what we've failed to do the thing
Can't grasp this confluence of widget & plasma

— makes our nation potent.

•

But for infantry you've offered
To hold my hand & in it
Place the name for something

Else say clarity for darkness say
Ditch for house or sky
A whole world in exchange

For foxholes and poetry
Equals this one defeat being
In the future perfect meaning

                    — you will have been already dead.

•

Twice yr dying came by steel
As nail from iron made of doubt
Driven won in wood we have

Wrested disbelief from things
Can't speak of sky and boys
Beyond belief my thing cries out

Of glass the labor a stone my bone
What's never here for having been
Penetrated by things impenetrable

Yr cock a thing I still can't say

— *no in good faith.*

To make the other sky this
Sky being a thing we've failed
To do having survived our own

Survival of the one failing sky
The dead this time will bury
Themselves & their graves

— will look like my house.

●

— and minus this place

The passion that old parousia a body limp inside a self
Dreaming itself there in the cold present one's own
Labor fails to make futures rather issues stony

Dysphorias on the dining room floor being
My impenetrable stools

— so prosodic and inoperative.

•

When yr home radiates my longing to be fucked
By prosthesis of that other sky say the boy or his leg
Blown away by contracts this fact being endurable

Becomes the unendurable engine singing of hygiene
And glamour being good but how lonely the nail
His palm the fingers my asshole leaves little

— hope for doubt.

•

Having been no longer one
- self no longer being a body
In a foxhole in a friend
Yr body it's like that sky

Or a ditch whose boy could be
A whole new structure of space
My house without nail no word

— and surely this will not have been this.

•

This being what I may have touched in you
Where stone and stone will never touch yr
Hole will never enter rock can't say rock

Nor tree tree and still there's nothing to see
Neither stone nor sky nor wood nor house
Nor any bird in most circumstances would

Be sufficient to initiate the naming w/
Nothing nameable now I'm not I
Mean what will have been

Here if there were
Something just
Say

— *here.*

•

— *where*

There will have been no ditch
No sky under such raptures
Of skin of infantry or whatever

Envelops explosions of sense
Whose only word for here remains

— *remains.*

•

Distances domestic and sidereal begin to hang
And blur the radiant materials begin to think
For themselves they act and leap and fuck

These things on me being fate
- less starless a suspended re
- ach and reaching out

For realer me
- asures to
Touch you

— nail   wood   sky

Whose knowledge bears no light.

NOTES ON AFFECTION AND WAR

— stuff my heart with moss and watch the
wounded boy moaning by the water —

•

My body keeps channeling so many contradictory feelings around the figure of a soldier *intensity of shame* as his body becomes the object of my violence and my lust. I want to kill him for blocking my dream of a demilitarized future, and I want to be fucked by him because the repressive sublimation of his body has become unbearable, the way the realization that I, too, stand in the way of that other future has become unbearable.

•

I don't know how I became aware of the militarization of common sense, or when it penetrated all my rhythms. Unavailable to immediate sensation *despite having pierced my senses* can I even be aware of this militarization now?

•

Lyric's nonsite *a place we can't perceive haunting everything we can* may be a military base *base of a soldier's balls* or a soldier's wound, this void in perception, fate of all that is common.

•

I don't know how to sing this, but I don't know how *not* to sing this either.

•

Walt Whitman offers a troubling model for singing what I can not *not* sing. "Affections shall solve the problem of freedom yet," he writes in "Over the Carnage Rose Prophetic a Voice." Longing, shame, fear, tenderness, rage, sorrow: the affections Whitman arouses in *Drum-Taps* require a battlefield for their full expression, a site where one's tenderness for a fallen soldier — "my comrade I wrapped in his blanket, enveloped well his form," etc. etc. — may be the most powerful affection of all.

•

Whatever organs wherein these affections are stimulated and trapped *aroused and neutralized* already bear the scars of the other future they block.

•

Whitman arouses so many intimacies in his democratic vista *mythic future of my country, extension of a mangled present* seemingly raw at first, unbound to any proper social knowledge. The open form of feeling in the Civil War verses organizes an emergent sound — "the hum and buzz of the great shells" — echolocating inchoate feeling tones *fear shame sorrow tenderness rage* whose sub-vocal expression *Drum-Taps* goes on to marshal as purposeful emotion. In doing so, Whitman performs the affective tuning of a military figure, a sound figure perhaps only fully realized in our own present. This tuning has naturalized my ears, so I can't hear the noise any longer, a silence we might now call completed sound, converging with its own suppression.

•

"Affections shall solve the problem of freedom yet." To organize prosodically an experience of the war, Whitman links uncoded affects, say, a certain unsingable tenderness for a dead soldier's body — "I bend down and touch lightly with my lips the white [*sic*] face in the coffin" — to over-coded attachments *love of nation, fervor for democracy* whereby our desire to be affected *this need to feel something that feels real* gets contracted to a nation whose intelligibility those same feelings have the potential to disrupt and undo.

•

If prosody is organized stress *technology for making meaning out of rhythm and sound* then Whitman is a masterful technician. His prosodic audition organizes the enclosure and containment of the "hum and buzz," a sound that could, if untuned and unleashed, disrupt the militarization that makes it audible. What might that untuning sound like? How might this sound sound from the impossible horizon of a demilitarized world, and from there, what will we have heard *here*?

•

Like sensation, prosody is always exceeding the structures available to contain its organization, or like an organ of cognition in the process of theorizing its own historical disaster, or like a body communicating in excess of its rhetorical gestures.

•

Even while prohibiting it, military culture stimulates homoerotic affection in just proportion with a paranoid disavowal of its usefulness. It's a textbook illustration of "instinctual renunciation," whereby the prohibition of eros becomes the site of erotic satisfaction. By contrast, Whitman affirms the use of homoerotic affection while still pressing it into the service of nation building. His homoerotic comradeship *partisan and militant* becomes fraternal mourning *unaligned and disarmed* as soon as comrade becomes soldier. [1]

•

Whitman's prosodic drive toward a postwar democracy is contra-dictory *not unlike my own* and quietly harbors militarized sense, at once ahistorical *prescribing amnesia* and metaphysical *positing value.* This desire for democracy requires a sacrifice, a body that disappears *withdrawn from view* just as it achieves a sublime meaning. *How to restore that thing to the relations from which it's been absented?* To be that sacrificial body, a soldier's corpse is drained of its historicity *bare life, dead meat, taboo* just as the nation's mourning is hygienically cleansed of partisan *militant* subjectivity.

•

If a body *any body* can become a vehicle for state security *aggression and defense* what might it mean to give the body up to insecurity, vulnerability, risk? What might it mean to suspend a proprietary relation to one's body in the interest of "common wealth" *poverty and love*? This ideal may be perversely realized in the figure of the soldier *self-immolation in the interest of public contracts* or whenever being naked means deadly exposure to shrapnel and debt.

•

Despite whatever delusion of mastery, the soldier's body is a *patient* body, informed equally by what it can do and by what can be done to it: at once the agent of dispossession and the patient of an expropriated common. Given over to the reigning sense of public good *security money carnage* the soldier's body materializes a fundamental ambivalence, its militarized agency *prosthetic of state power* being paradoxically a function of that body's *patiency*.

•

I'm evoking the soldier as neither a thing nor an idea, but rather a relation *like capital like value* visible and measurable only in the effects it achieves and the affects it arouses.

•

The poems of Whitman's *Drum-Taps* make our implication in the production *love* of these *our* militarized bodies palpable. Arousing intimate sensations, the poems yoke the affects they stimulate to contrary ends, channeling the reader's feelings while coding *redeeming* our relation to carnage. It's at this redemption that my poems rage.

•

All my queer affections, like those aroused in Whitman's poems, are used *like sap like cum* to bind our national interests, even as I refuse them.

•

Long before Whitman mobilized tender emotions for national interests, Virgil, in book IX of the *Aeneid*, tells the story of two soldier-lovers: Euryalus "renowned for handsomeness and for his fresh youth," and Nisus, who "burned for Euryalus with chaste love."

•

Inquiring into the source of their passion, Nisus asks:

'Euryalus, is it
the gods who put this fire in our minds,
or is it that each man's relentless longing
becomes a god to him? Long has my heart
been keen for battle or some mighty act;
it cannot be content with peace or rest.'

While the first two lines read as an expression of desire that the two men feel for each other, the passage resolves that desire in a longing for "mighty acts." Virgil amazes me with his manner of arousing two kinds of "fire" — amorous and martial — which are then rhetorically fused. Semantic registers collide and pederastic affection becomes a lubricant for the work of war and empire building. Erotic body and murderous body are inseparable, the one becoming a vehicle of transport, motivating and propelling the other: "Their minds and hearts were one / in war they charged together." [2]

•

How to unbind this eros from martial interests, wrest an openness to penetration away from sovereign ends? How to disentangle my desire from a long genealogy of homoerotic camaraderie embedded in histories of empire and nation, but without denying these entanglements? How to sing of affections unrelated to a legacy of internecine exploits, to arouse the aimless aims of eros in advance of the categories available to harness them? [3]

•

Feelings become socially useful before they can be improperly felt. Fear, shame, lust, tenderness, rage, sorrow: these affects are public and historical, the raw material of social emotion before it hardens in foreclosed identities, voices and values capable of perverting the violence they otherwise arouse and lubricate. But when perceived as private, intimate, and personal, these same affects quietly serve my grotesque war economy.

•

What might it sound like to subtract my affections from the wars to which they have been unwittingly contracted? I can't hear this sound. I can't make this sound. *I need to hear this sound. I need to make this sound.* How to register all the distortions, frustrations, and amplifications that fallout in the effort to lend a sound figure to this inaudibility?

•

I want to undo this usefulness, to abject these feelings by stimulating their unmastered remains *emotive waste of a carnage that ought to be finished but is still beginning again and again and again* to activate these affections before they become integral to reproducing a structure of unending war.

•

This is the story of how my love goes bad in the body of a soldier.

•

The soldier embodies an obstruction *this obsessive recurrence* as my poems struggle against the grain of common sense to perceive what a demilitarized world might feel like *his hard muscle being what's in the way.*

•

To make contact with his wounds, the seduction being that of reference itself *nothing but this language* at once proffered and denied.

•

As for Whitman's vision, the affections unleashed on the battlefield become in his poems the material for a perverse social alchemy whose transcendent yield would be nothing short of freedom itself. "The continuance of Equality shall be comrades," he writes in "Over the Carnage." But Whitman's vision of a post-Civil War restored America, free and democratic, requires a very particular fallen body *my homonational* whose eros silently fills the hushed space between my organs, otherwise drowned in unheard war noise.

•

The body required to ensure the nation's vision of freedom and democracy is a dead one *note the nimbus around his withdrawn corpse, function of pure exchange* an aneurism in the present, a clot of volatile affects wrested from the pathos of meaning his body inspires *in me, even now.* What would it sound like to hear that clot rupture in a poem struggling to adapt in advance to the conditions of a world we've failed to make?

•

A bleeding guy in uniform, fallen guarantor of America's future: what feelings does this body conduct, and how might they be organized differently, if only to arouse Whitman's homoerotic affections otherwise, to pervert them from their militarized ends *the police, being the future of this democracy?*

•

Aura concentrates in the figure of this fallen soldier *so attractive so repulsive*. Sometimes he's barely perceptible *stalking the periphery of all I see* but always available for contrary ends *fundamental ambivalence of the body*. A whole metaphorics of love and war *my phalynx of clichés* converge around his vulnerability to penetration.

•

"O the bullet could never kill what you really are, dear friend / Nor the bayonet stab what you really are" (Whitman). Needle, finger, tongue, cock, shrapnel, none of these things will ever penetrate *kill* what my soldier really is, being beyond reach. Bodies lubricate the war, but the soldier's body becomes a hole in sense, and just as it begins to hemorrhage, it contracts transcendent value *the nation, freedom being what you really are*.

•

I want to undo Whitman's militarized vision *democracy fulfilled* by betraying its perversity. And yet my poems become evermore distorted, frustrated and perverted in the process *turned away from their impossible aim* because their own utopian longings are blocked by current conditions under which a demilitarized world is inconceivable *depressing conclusion of this research*. I want my writing to move in the fault where desire *the body* collides with those conditions, and where the poems might become sensory organs in the process of perceiving this situation in ways my mind can't yet conceive or sense.

•

The hard bodies of all these soldiers at war bear the sign of my consent if only because my dissenting voice *like my writing* has done nothing to stop those wars. This inspires my rage, my lust, my shame, so many queer feelings coursing thru a national agenda that can include them all *democracy* in its effort to consolidate the meaning of all those other others forever excluded *terrorist immigrant criminal.*

•

The body at war *extension of these affections* open to risk without tenderness, penetration without pleasure: the body as purest meat, the nation's consensual pulse. The hole a weapon makes, where global processes *accumulation by dispossession, neoliberal austerity, environmental degradation, profitable incarceration* collide with the body's intimate recesses *all my desires and repulsions* externalized, obdurate and opaque to my cognition. Residues of living labor congeal in such bodies where love hardens with the muscle *interpenetration of corpus and finance.*

•

Or, the 'I' congeals and hardens the way my cock hardens in a soldier's wound, this being an asymptotic limit, figural horizon, ludicrous conceit *obsessive ridiculous perverse* which shapes a gesture, limns an imaginary site *would that it were only perceptible* where all the affects and feelings aroused in penetration congregate, awaiting transfiguration.

•

Bullet hole, foxhole, asshole: openings thru which our common product enters and exits *like my mouth* and where Whitman submits his sweet affections to an empire's emergence. Without indulging any false identification *superimposition* of these incommensurate holes, I'm compelled by the thread that moves thru them *my poem's line.*

•

The line moves thru song and soldier whose body has been immunized *withdrawn used wasted denied* a body in which the *munus* — a gift from nowhere and belonging to no one, gift of openness, risk, and vulnerability — has been refused *rejection of unanticipated care* as if such refusal might defend a larger social body against unanticipated penetration. But in claiming immunity, one concedes the terms whereby the body remains already contracted to its own death *this immortality of which we die in droves.*

•

To negate the soldier, then, by restoring this body to unthinkable relation *rematerialize a dematerialized sensuousness* to return the immune to community, to render the body as site of common refusal:

refusal of transcendent property (identity, enclosures, contracts); refusal of self-preservation (the death drive in disguise); refusal of hardened borders (the uneven distribution of vulnerability).

•

Can my poem make audible the unheard sound of passing into this demystified form of social relation, or can it only harbor the clot of relation's thwarted energies?

•

What might it sound like to sing so that song might loosen this clot: to activate a pornographic imagination against the militarized common sense that has otherwise fully harnessed it, and to unbind those affects otherwise sclerotically bound to the nation's ends? What might it feel like to perceive this unbinding in a poem that also registers the obstructions to these utopian longings? I want to situate the poem on a threshold where such sensations stand a chance of becoming perceptible, but I don't know where such a threshold is because only the poem can sense it.

1 // As Cristanne Miller notes, the 1865 edition of *Drum-Taps* hews closely to a Union ideology where it is nothing less than "democracy" as such that is threatened by the Civil War. Miller reads the 1865 edition against the later redaction and incorporation of the sequence in the 1871 edition of *Leaves of Grass* and notes how the 1865 edition records Whitman's partisanship with respect to an idealized democracy, as well as his support for a US free of slavery, while holding on to all the prewar values that inform the great 1855 edition of *Leaves of Grass* — individual liberation, at once erotic and political, thru collective liberty — despite the emerging contradiction within those values made manifest by the war. By 1871, however, Whitman's investment in the Civil War — or a story of the war — includes his belief in the war's protection of a never defined "democracy" that required a new form of fraternal mourning as a practice of national reconciliation. Here I'm assuming a longer view of the transformation of *Leaves of Grass* whereby Whitman's 1855 vision of social cohesion thru a fully embodied eros becomes a re-vision of national reunion the aims of whose eros are to bind the community in the figure of a wounded or dead soldier. In other words, the later sequence called "Drum-Taps" affirms precisely what the war questioned: the very possibility of a sustainable US democracy. See Christanne Miller, "Drum-Taps: Revisions and Reconciliation," *Walt Whitman Quarterly Review* 26 (Spring 2009) 171-196.

2 // Jean Genet offers a very different model for rendering these affections, one that blocks redemption at every turn. Working thru the death of his lover — a resistance fighter who died on the barricades in the final days of WWII — almost a century after Whitman, the narrator of *Funeral Rites* writes, "My pain was so great that it sought escape in the form of fiery gestures: kissing a lock of hair, weeping on a breast, pressing an image, hugging a neck, tearing out grass, lying down on the spot and falling asleep in the shade, sun, or rain with my head on my bent arm. What gesture

would I make? What sign would be left me?" The extremity of loss seeks repose in the seemingly familiar movements of a body *is it kitsch? is it melodrama?* where meaning concentrates in excess of the signs that would make those movements intelligible. No one gesture will ever be sufficient, but each suggests an ephemeral choreography communicating beyond its rhetorical moves. The death of the narrator's lover is a death whose meanings — national, political, social — swarm in excess of any one story, and Genet's narrative functions to make those meanings unavailable for any sanctioned use beside his own disfigured grief.

3 // On one of our long walks, my friend Marc Schachter drew my attention to this passage, which illustrates the inverse of those narratives within the male friendship tradition that cite homoerotic affection as a necessary hedge *against* a corrupt politics (tyranny). The locus classicus here is Pausanias's speech in Plato's *Symposium:* "Indeed this thing [pederasty], along with philosophy and the pursuit of physical education, is shameful to foreigners on account of their tyrannical governments. For, I think, it is not useful to rulers for great ambitions to be born in those ruled, nor strong friendships or fellowships, which all these things but mostly love are pre-eminently apt to create. Indeed, the tyrants in our country learned this by experience, for the love of Aristogiton and the friendship of Harmodius grew so strong that it utterly destroyed their rule." Marc comments on this passage brilliantly in his book *Voluntary Servitude:* "In Pausanias's account, pederasty produces citizens who are not amenable to tyrannical rule because, above all else, the love of boys engenders ambition, friendship and fellowship in its practitioners. For this reason, foreigners under despotic sway are opposed to pederasty, along with philosophy and training at the gymnasium, because they have similar results. Thus, for Pausanias, the *erotic* voluntary servitude he champions in pederasty also has a political dimension. It facilitates the production of citizens who will refuse the yoke of *political* voluntary

servitude, or tyranny . . . When Pausanias contends that his version of virtuous pederasty is antithetical to tyranny he is paradoxically asserting that erotic servitude, which would itself be effeminizing, leads to political liberty." He goes on to note how Jacques Derrida, in *The Politics of Friendship*, avoids addressing the implications of a specifically pederastic eros of passivity in Plato's *Symposium*, focusing his critique instead on a certain "sublime 'virile homosexuality,'" as if the agential aspect of male friendship alone were of critical value within the genealogy of a "democracy to come." Derrida thereby occults a potentially more radical eros of penetrability, vulnerability, and patiency. Most interesting for me in Marc's discussion is the way it puts certain masculinist assumptions regarding an overvalued agency — *virility* — into question within the rhetorics and imaginaries of "democracy." I can't help but wonder how Whitman's Civil War poems both extend and belie Pausanias's argument, given how the penetrated body becomes, in war, a dead one. See Marc Schachter, *Voluntary Servitude and the Erotics of Friendship* (Burlington: Ashgate Publishing, 2008).

RUNAWAY SOLDIER PUNK

Y — yeah! Ungh! Ungh! Ungh! Get
ready for yr master's hot baby, punk!
Watch it, I'm gonna shoot —

Not yet, he said, still groping, tonguing
upper body strength, rippling hollow
and torquing roughly down about the
knees, twisting, sensing

— sorry, I'm just desperate to see the
spirit coming, choking back my sobs of
pain and tender humiliation.

NONSOUND, A MUSICAL

No song onsite these airs sing what things
Can't be needs forgotten grafted manes
To metal scored hews whose breath resides
In place where matter voided voices still

The things I've abolished beat down ears
With instruments plump dealers produce
Extracted breath by force returns tones
Sound silence dead in a cavity my mouth

Collects their parts in words bones graft
Lives undo deeds themselves struck out
Downed subjects don't matter by accord
Threat menace refuse no living sounds re

- sidues breath resides in anthem noise
Choppers ammo floods a sky not being
Sky and the sea's vast plains whose military
Sonics sew the ground what we produce

Trains ears on spectral sounds surround
Us systems sing in private mouths deeds
Force airs menace ears metal tones things
We've muted living hums blown bits into

Them being bone ash all our dead remains
Residual song refusing clings to breath
Wrecked mouths tubes absent horns beats

— silence onsite, a music we never hear.

SO BRAVE A BEGINNING AS THIS

These days the difference being kind
Of hazy whose eros settles a fine dust
Objects being mine to kill the waste

Makes me pretty unsure of being sub
- ject to what I think I'm feeling when I
Am feeling anything at all my affections

Assume strange shapes round intractable
Violence so exquisite the bodies these e
- masculated young men manned by wan

- ton desires felled squires dead the wound
- ed whose bodies I've never seen so much
Open flesh renowned handsomeness o

- cculted friends who burn in war ardent a
- micum berserk with lust being ours to fuck
Fresh youth all honest minds & hearts be

\- ing one we sleep together doing inadvert

\- ent service for empire long before the sun

Being no friend to nocturnal comrades

Secret lovers thrust force pierce ribs his

Tongue tied in blood stained mouth

— my purple flower, severed by the plow.

FOR THE GOOD LIFE

This culture of the heart it's what I want
To give you an inflated idea of myself so
- mething unrecognizable or an image of it
Being this innate propensity of things

To be evasive I kissed his cock a bit he
Took umbrage broke my branded organ
With no future yr floating lines make me
Really hot like direct address there's al-

Ways a soldier getting off in the wings
Where nothing can come in from out
There except the words they keep things
Coming wherever new industry is wel

- come I keep digging for you to see
Time make my body delirious w/ trade
Whose skin fails to name whatever's in
It making missiles & houses for the good

Life equals what the army guys know
They're gonna snap but if I could
Only kiss a few more like you

> *— my song might have real weight.*

INTO THIS SUSPENDED VACUUM

for John Wieners

Whatever militates against our dreamier pleasures I have
Become the same meaning utopia's crude petroleum jolts
Coded rubber heat singing things that turn blind eyes to waste
Erasing worlds being serial resolves my fate in theory I think

I want to love and loving kiss yr many addled hallucinations
Hunger fulfillment's no longer a glamour hangs dependence
On feeding the thing eternally expressing selves in public
Johns voices saying before you decide to leave me leave

Me a rag some hair a duct or mass producing anything external
Can't arouse thus corrodes the tongue with news I can't be
Warm or think my own repression cause it's too hot inside this
War to dream communications a soiled body nobody wants

To express can't be itself in goods another total embracing
Wants to believe belief enough to become the world we can't

— ~~cause the cops can't fucking fathom.~~

BATHED IN WAR'S PERFUME,
MY DELICATE RAG

If I could sing the dead uncomely
Tones don't issue sounds can't hear
Torn things tear whose pain's a pun
Where no one's body is I can be

Seen for shame whole nations
Leaven big inside my loins mon
- uments remains assume this shape
O sleeping boy but for the stain

Still spreading thru yr lap there is
Warmth the sun keeps me feeling
So very far away —

      still watching you my tan-faced
Soldier at some remove a gaze re

- cessed inside sunken eyes no longer
Seeing I feel mounting my mourning
Telepathic powers signal this mon
- umental failure of my freedom

              — *to see you.*

REMAINS UNWRITTEN

My own stench being what attracts me
To undressing you mean what I think I
-'m feeling dismembered in the touch

I still can't touch or say the names fall out
For what's not mine to name you softer
Targets yrs I want to sing what will have

Been my body where yr odor clings I hang
In excess of the system where we're caught

> — *not sensing the thing that's sensing us.*

WHAT DELUSIONS OF YR PRICE

Yr mind being that of the mark
- et it's not the secret of yr body
I want but the secret of value be

- ing the thing itself or what
Mystery connects me

> — *to the world.*

SKIN FLICK

Yr belly's hard but I'm soft
And tho soft may be good
For something I can't say what

Corrodes my words the world
Being whatever yr mouth sings
Inside me still smaller pieces

Blown bones and contracts

                    — form my just opinion.

THIS ORGAN OPENS
ONE TO STRUCTURE

The situation's pretty unstable
Said my soldier with no hands
And I imagine his prosthetic

Up my ass I love the feeling I
Even quiver with the pleasure
Of being

                        — *so near the goal.*

MY OPERATIVES

War yet shall be, but warriors — are now but operatives.
— Melville

Now that I've addressed the soldier *luminous*
Flesh all erotic mastery an anvil-din a wholeness
Comes upon me in this moment's dull emergency
A blank in the social fabric a police action now

Gone missing sanctioned with the halo of event
Open rents whose spirit pisses peoples my own
Shattered aspect jumbled shards fly valued dress
Dolled up the coded elements lift me even higher

Gestures fly yr fisticuffs lend identity a pounding
To all our dutiful goods how can we not have this
Paranoid relation to the names themselves eternal
Things screw truths into such stunning parks let's

Go there holding hands and touching even more
Than every soldier names us out beyond the war
Perception's reach I mean I'm the war's perception
What can't be heard inside me calculations of caloric

The only real event this thing impossible to prove
Took place & goes on reaching for me my history
Being one of these different ways of killing things
To access what my body's become yr private waste

Exquisite feeling hard clots sound the ministrations
Unsanctioned activity diddling more than ever now
Various and vague designs pump meaner things up
In our lung sacks as if other worlds were nigh whose

Common forms remain unseen to bomb her baby
This will have secured me here

— still longing for yr hair.

•

Now that we've undressed the soldier all my
Damp embarrassments sticky limbs stuffed in
Sacks his poor thing triumphed in an afterglow
Of poverty and shame a mutilated blank opaque

He's crapped spread eagle reveals what others
Refuse sells more events bigger targets dumps
Fail to happen precisely onsite is nowhere some
Ghostly void or dead zone around my body

Collects a hyaline film and my mucous hardens
Yielding new sugars upon decomposition sordid
Shapes assume their own lost objects memories
Of his hair the old gunner stained with eosin some

Thing they call experience for lack of any other
Idea of what happens to bone under war stress
Cathects yr thinking to my song twists love's
Caresses yearn to correspond with what destroys

Identity's torn apart so it's catastrophe that holds
Us together now that we've suppressed every other
Unexplained abused convulsion the very acts we
Disavow some things do happen addressing boys

Ourselves allows me to make believe I still want
My nudity neat absolute without value our skin
Contracts inside any residual content a filmy gloss
Of chemic aims splintered elements yr own

Oppositional remnants wasted turds scarred even
This holds my tongue inside yr immeasurable

— *gulf to be defiled.*

•

Now that we've caressed the soldier I can finally
Touch myself again begging to be called the names
He used to call himself when the nation loved
His bloodstool eating it and fucking them singing

Is it in yet yes yes you can do it in the barest light
Of reason where cruel names find proper realization
And what you wear is how they eat little over there
Where the land is one with its things & peoples don't

Make me yr fall guy he said *I am you* when it's dark
Our own failure to happen is the only event worth
Noting phases sucking off a self-defining absence
Of content can't you see I'm already my own worst

Formalism all the marrow sucked out of everything
Lick yr own wounds it said as if the words would make
Me one with the current traumatic neuroses of peace
That's how we live on waste he said crawling out

Under the dead weight a carcass had come rising
When he saw me on my knees his dick in my mouth
Creaming him crushed beneath the weight of nations
Lost thinking what will this joy do to my tongue how

Will I call things back now this is sadness my friend
Bob calls it the unbearable sorrow of having no future
In the present and tho he had something else in mind
I'm thinking

                          — *about what he said now.*

•

Now that we've seduced the soldier my own thought
Thins to a fevered nought there never having been before
The war things were identical whereas now difference
Reigns in names for annihilation being mine own peace

And stability industry ricochets and ducks the largest
Private army a one man truth squad alone dodging total
Intelligence solutions chop off surveillance blings dry
Ice flights cross central Asia under contract with the gov't

But that was under Clinton and we're in a peace industry
Now folks in high places water specialists monitors witness
Largest private army rapidly approaching our convoy
Ducks beneath detection to a point a heavy wire fence be-

Hind which I'm hiding with my pants down down around
The ankles aren't clean none of it's clean and not much
Is really any good any more but I'm still coming to love
And will wait there

— *being no 'before the war' anymore.*

•

Now that we've embarrassed our meat man
A hammered cavity banged up bad with fierce
Repetition all the ammo dumped down deep
Into the vast and criminal abyss I don't mean his

Belly is what we sleep with their cheeks all wet
With blood and piss and the steam rising from
What heat amounts to when his wig's found out
Of curl and loses its phosphorescence this being

— my only proper sun.

GREAT ARMIES OF THE WOUNDED

So come again my troops no
- iseless mists vapors gather
Round me boys phantoms all

Fragments of a mobile space
Seared with our metaphysics
Of service & reserve the sold

- iery loves me trading what
The war heats up it offers
Worlds of feeling very deep

Much deeper than defiance all
Slain things being equal wealth
Bodies fucked real deep inside

— the nation's gorgeous booty.

•

My soldier my odalisque my
Fossil of trade pressing thru
Yr face an explosion of sense

Penetrates skin a landscape
Itself a catastrophe blowing up
A head somewhere inside

It being this dream of life

— coming in my hotel bathroom.

•

Nothing I can see from here equals
His impossible form all riddled w/
Their holes & pasted viscera travel

Far as value lives inside the dead
Things tagged a skin becomes this
Organ my hand moist intimate

— *recess.*

•

Soldiers bodies gorgeous the
Thighs I want to gaze at them
What stumps old carbines be

- hold how things ignore me
His thighs being all but vacant
Names our commonplace en

- closing so many oppositions
Ours theirs being wooly sex so
Much wooly sex under vast blue

A vast blue blanket being for

          — or against what yr woolen skivvies give.

•

Following close upon his body
Parts stuff the marts of wealth I
Get moist for friendship means

All these guys ignite my love
With objects parsing lands them
- selves sleeves a soldier dumped

     — *his dead in me.*

•

Yr skivvies sing among others
Linking all my little feints blown
Thru target locations mangled bone

Attitudes of duty & debt esoteric
Securities fundamentalist pop
- ulisms negating politics like so

Many little negotiations of private
Interest embalmed with my love
My poems service you as well as

Waste demands what's deepest re
- mains a delicate pumping sensation
Feeling this can't mean this

     — difference hasn't yet begun.

•

Voids in perception a nation hangs
Its futures tagged in graves unheard
Phonemes burial-squads screaming
For delicacies he calls my organs

Oranges strung-out on jellies fruit
Tobacco a whole white nakedness
His moaning mourns a man like
Belief I write these things inside

— *yr address myself enclosing.*

●

A badly dubbed audio his lips
Arouse my skin a canopy a sel
- ving sleeves inside a frame

Contriving recovery it's so patriotic
Duty crushed a head in my groin
Puffed up on the unidentified

Airs nothing real no experience
To speak of nothing to sing
These poems just keep coming

       — this disease of my mouth.

LOVE SONG (TO MY FALLEN SOLDIER)

Kissing you I get hard inside all the export containers
Being such an excess of relation filling these negations
Of relation it's so antagonistic purity being a thing
Like what I'm called when I love him and the love just

Limps it limps inside yr groin's the place I want to call
My real location at nite when the belly's all hot my limbs
Beat over ocean fantasies more militant boys spilling up
Into air it's commercially endless the flows and the ships

Refurbished canisters vacant homes having descended
To us from the surd state what with no noise yr moan it's
But an adjunct of sound compressed inside every cell
Walls can't contain the bloody stumps guys like you have

To cover up yr privates over there where their remains
Make a people of us having been left over by this unin
- terrupted series of interruptions at nite it's like rubbing
Up against my neighbor's hard earned metal while sucking

Off the troops whole catastrophes of skin his foot stuck in-
Side my head bears no sign no trace of these promiscuous
Chambers our secrets stacked high on the docks our trade
Imbalance has given me a lot more room for fucking where

Wouldn't we be if we weren't really here making history hot
Markets I can't see you being held in a pen projecting dim
- inishing returns on all our precious objects they've been
Reduced to stones their image being a hole in yr face

Or a hood over the sky my negative element *o qualitas*
Occulta! with no escaping primary nature we're all just
So many blown limbs our interiors can't contain all the
Traffic in oversea exchange we shrink into beautiful

Fantasies bodies piling up inside enclosures once I was
Caught where ambushes & hampers bloom and interspe
- ciation favors new unities of spirit and matter while the
Nucleus of time crystallizes in a lug way down deep inside

My soldier's groin goes deeper still one shot right thru
His bladder a hole in my face no one can see the body's
A force a capacity to heal now there's no placc for them
The sanctioned containers replacing our displacement

One practice at a time you can be my little explosive de
- vices ensure the singular thing thru which my poem keeps

        — singing of shit, and all yr hemorrhaging affections.

MEMORANDA

— being descriptions of soldiers and war impressions
in memo form, often from notes taken on the spot —

That a body could be a real frontier. Strewn in fields of waste, organs sensing under siege, mere shadow cast of value, a hardened rind, or money form, whatever remains when you stop believing in it. A false membrane, a whole catastrophe of skin, the thickness of these accidents. One small annulus, a floating hole in *phynance* radiates my longing to be fucked under soldier's sun. Now's the time, he says, humping hard my thigh, dreaming the coming reign of poverty and love. There's ground for what this can't contain, yr swollen excess, gummy extension of a self rising like a hand from sand and slag, a glassy pink appearance, a hyaline veneer, looming just above the mouth. Feeding on pure product, poems and esoteric securities, harvesting my field of corpse & shit. Crouching on the overpass, dreaming tight schedules of outgoing cargo flights, smuggling weapons to a desert in Chad. Cunning plans to colonize the dead, these feelings I'm still marshalling, tender affections harnessed to bad information and its real registration on a body I'll never see go down. Long before his brain's pronounced dead, I hear the thing has already occurred, so I visualize his innermost organ, this impression of truth, the signs that bloat his swollen thing. The landscape delinks me from every trace of physical trauma, nothing to reverse this unbearable lag in my productivity. Whose paranoia tastes like real meat anyway. I'm a mere police operation now, taking charge of biosphere and mulch, no services left to support our secret plan. But we've been very busy, harvesting the cup-like ascoma, so bulbous at the base, wondering how to transport our new object into fields of visionary prospect without turning up on screen ourselves. If I could only anatomize the sovereignty that's made itself continuous with a body language has all but abandoned. Instead, we work undercover in the cool aluminum shade, anodized, shot-penned and learning, still learning how to throw the simultaneity of these synchronized measures (differentiation, correction, punishment, waste) on a linear axis, plotting whose enjoyment of all my body's functions. At this point, anything will do to advance our counter-purposes, the secret of the thing being that it has no secret.

Turning our attention to the ground, this stately film of thought, all the body bags and rime, whatever burns a shuddering reason, trade winds suspend me in a mindless blow. How about a little cheap *frisson*, he says, thinking there'll be pleasure in my void. Anything for more soldier fuck, I mean there's aura in yr beauty, encoded bliss, so much atrium and palm. My arms will never be my own, he says, and I nod consolingly, considering the time between his thighs, the hanging lags, such deep bogs of it, what pleasure and procured resource. I was curious as to the shape of his avail, but dissatisfaction fell in its wake, as if all we'd harvested — all the blowsy brown-skins, the little bits of bone and teeth — could ever graft a future to so much absence of tense. It all gets lost in the semblance of our shedding. Dashing into a desert hut to filch a flask of fuel, I conceal every sign of my arousal, all the eczema and hair. If we could only disrupt the hold of all these Latinate words and become more Saxon. Everything we stand for, everything we do, it all bears sickness *o what sweetness in his scent!* foul winds of crime, and scattered traces of the next deluge. Experiencing vague intimations of anal pleasure makes it all worthwhile, but they've successfully dissuaded me from mentioning that. Becoming instead these massive blocks of sound, my own staged effect, disaster relief and soaring rates. What abstruse details define us (partnership income & capital gains) and what conditions make them so (market dysphoria & a captive electorate of white rural voters). Cross-checking all the symptoms in breviaries and grammars, I try to catalogue these fears, connect every stutter to some aspect of the war. This issues a recitation of old lists, all the minerals and plantations, nickel and tobacco extracted from a narrow base, and other signs of insured wealth. A drop in wages diverts us from futurity, brings it back to 'suspend me in a mindless blow.' Why crop so grim a feel, he says, just bring on the tethered yoke and dust, seal the ordnance with sperm and plasma. But it's all too frightening when the thickening trace grows animate. So we shelter these imagined habitations, vision of homes now gone, collops of the shameful flesh grown thin with hut.

B oarding a bus to tour the devastation, a spontaneous surge
of meaning irrupts inside the grid. A blackening corpuscle,
an indecipherable glyph, ruin lurks deep in the bowels, my
poem's stupid plan, a wasting syndrome, this place without history.
Yr body without my mouth, it's mere environment, but with my
tongue it becomes territory. Fingers rim whose feint like tears.
A stain without limit, his dead weight adds a lot of drag to our
lateral glide. Moving in a halo of shame, the love of a militiaman,
democracy's soul, a thing that fails to happen, suspended in this
mindless blow, incalculable interval where we almost make contact
with the present. Singing in the fault of our temporal divide, who
will have been here to hear this. *Mon petit soldat, mon semblable* yr
touch makes me other than the meat I am. Yrs can be the soft part,
a loaf's spongy middle, a place we have no name for. With this in
mind, after removing blindfolds and cuffs, I push the bodies into a
canal before joining other members of the unit waiting in a nearby
truck, ready to return to the post. Remains erase the ones whose
names we'll never sing. The fact that they don't have access to the
river nor the authority to dig their own wells hasn't been explicitly
mentioned, and while conspicuous signs do trickle thru the wire
mesh, it's not enough to derail our program. This decay of sound, the
way capital wiggles, a worm in my stool. Thick description replaces
the self with rumors of a clean interior. Wire and cranes, rebar and
concrete, it's all been gathered after the war for repackaging. Just
watch me disinfect in creepy mist. Patches of heather here and

there, thistle, columbine, and rose, such dreams of beauty blanket space. Reducing appetite to forced withdrawal, we marvel at the thing's capacity, sublime, this magnitude of failing grip. Please, touch me here again. Consider these pared down phrases, how they fail to register the erosion of system-wide reference, while the recrudescence of all that remains identical with itself binds me in thrall to so many small conspiring forces, like steel, like corn. No doubt, you can compose an image of the damage by extrapolating freely from the glossy surface of my private's pretty face when his rectum opens, my cavernous abode, proverbial wound, inaudible diphthong in a dead Afghani's impossible name.

S unrise finds us touring disaster. No sun, and nothing true to fill its place. Voices draw attention to a dale — grotto, sea, or wood — as if any vista's sudden appearance, like a spell over spells, were but a function of our need to go on believing in it. My view is guaranteed by the bus. Yesterday, the situation arrived at its crisis, and tomorrow it will arrive again. Our current state being one of permanent interruption, this account appeals to a timeless suspension of the monetary form, already dissociated from its social base. Having grown accustomed to the abrogation of such acts *freedom of movement, freedom to farm* I imagine compensatory access to withdrawn life, the way money traces suppressed flows until motion comes to a standstill, the whole order arriving at equilibrium in dead labor. Try imagining another unified field model, he says, something not bound to the structure of carbon credit, anything to dispatch the false evidence of this false evidence. But I'm tethered to my corn, I think, regarding him there in some obscure light, half-naked, his erection, my murderous intent. Perhaps there's nothing more beautiful than this. Perforated light, so many dreamy holes, I want to believe the scheduled eclipse hasn't blinded me to what's still coming. I even want to play, despite the noisome sweat of my soldier's gorgeous wound. Everything's ok, he assures me, and I go on singing the relative value of his compromised body in coined equivalents, words to which all our negations have been reduced. Plying me with blandishments, prying me open, he pulls compass and string, plug and pump, out from a bedside pouch and introduces these things to our indecorous games. My body, a public feeling, a floating intensity no one can claim. You can put anything inside me, I want to say, anything to amplify these feelings of pity and shame, whatever it takes to help me get off. More refined techniques generate impressive indices of the war's most delicate pleasures. Take that Arab boy as an example, the one they reported dead in a ditch just outside a village whose name I can't pronounce. Beauty is a detour, like his tongue in my ass, a moment of grave remove, reflex of a system in love with its own reform. Drawing attention away from such seductions, all this occupies a panorama of once good urban living, guarantor of what the kill preserves in my flesh. Other zones fall in desuetude, but this poem has become all grass and birds, simple substitution for our ~~fear~~ sphere.

Out by the munitions dump, seeking shelter in a market driven sludge *what sunrise fullest feeds* hot ordnance bails out manholes for the money. My cock hardens in a soldier's wound. In the woods, beside the stalwart trees, the slender, tapering trees, we spot wild geese and many grasses, cite petroleum and timber, one vast and unobstructed flow. Self-evident affirmations cut false figures here. We recall all this upon trying to recall what's been happening out along the borders of our land and comprehension without wanting to compromise the mind, without wanting to piss on 'the sky is blue.' But really, I feel most myself upon entering the toilet on a transatlantic flight, where belief in the social aspect of all this goes down in soiled calculation. Finally alone to retrieve a little lost experience, something akin to the rational style of aid-giving, or at least my description of that. Traversing fields of mannered lights, having swallowed all the bulbs and cones, what corporate vapors illuminate our troops. My soldier wears a colored codpiece, anything to ensure the health of my mouth. A barely discernable supplement to the whole affair, like the decision to trade arms for hostages, or a split in the futures market, achieves the status of our lost foundation. Trussed in the alley of hemp and steel, my poems augment the other guy's pleasure. Slipping down concrete escarpments, shitting in a sea of yellow flags, this sudden lurching of my organ. With deafening noise, visions swell inside us, force transmission up the spine. Even the wind'll cut you down here, and to tree's a broken route. What terrific magnitudes of fluctuation.

Whether you accumulate or hoard, there's no committee on the docks, no sound from steel guitars. Imputing bodies where no one lives anymore, being the limit of our absorption, there's nothing more direct than this line to public safety. You can remain inactive, even be of inert substance and socially useless, and still be overproductive here. So we're just laying low in the margin for a while, examining the loquats, whatever hangs from blighted limbs, feeling kind of lost inside the unpretentious friendliness of yr people.

This report fails to confirm any experience at all, mere reenactment of the facts, and when I write *unmanned US drones form a hedge around our real impossibility* I'm not communicating in the true. Drawing near my lips, his bloated face. A fiscal edifice, can't feel my thing inside. Devouring eyes still summon, presiding over nations of receding flesh. As meanest meat, every body in history is mine. The moon, my stunted glow, touching purple limbs tossed wide. Pumping up the scene, full displays of public pleasure, utopian futures caked & glazed already. His body, my thing no longer bleeds. This is what happens when liberation coincides with total destruction, and the architecture reveals its sub-majestic aims. To be ploughed thru the stomach, the hole, like a half dollar, big enough for me to fully insert. Grabbing a pipe, I rush to dress his words, his wounds inside my mouth. What's it mean for my body not to be here, a memory of meat hung upon the self. Unable to distend, he hardens deep inside my calcified verse. *The nation has refused to die for you* echoes from a crappy wood. Lambent skin, translucent in a golden sun, my flag of teeming life, a screen to emphasize the void. Even the dirt of his humanity adds an inexplicable glow to the national sum, such allure to the skin. When I run my hand across his belly, unfolding now its delicate extreme, sensation reaches a point of unfamiliar intensity, such tremors of danger and joy, an enchanted domain against all odds, which opens to me its fortressed hedge, so strangely removed from our spectacle of terror. Testicles of error, dumped them on the side of a road, fantasies of scarcity becoming proper organ functions. Graft me to yr high rise slums and complementary flats. Whose cries now reversed, an ear curled up inside the throat. Airs sing upward from that cavity, anywhere to move beyond the old refrain of phantoms, this tangle of soldiers, bread and cash, coupling cynic airs to war songs. Fake soldiers, fucked soldiers, ripped immobile soldiers, perforated bags, whose bloody limbs could fill a bunghole. You are my self, a memory hung upon his corpse. Shot remains, full inside paradise, a refuse pail where I belong.

I can't fantasize about hot sex with soldiers the way I used to, and this is taking a toll on my writing. Gazing out on fields of prospect and demise, acknowledging old tree lines with perfunctory nods, barely tracking the thing beyond our diminished capacity to relate, my body lost inside the strudel of that thicket. Like a bag of shorn digits, it's all so supersensible. I run off with one and insert the thing fully, wondering whether I'll feel anything at all when I locate myself inside the dollarization of Ecuador and Peru. Feeling only phantom now, an inconsolable figure, a soldier's precious organ, a recycled impression on my processed affectionate core. I'm nothing but this raw material for military use. Otherness always resembles me a little too much for there to be any ethical possibility. The best way to end an occupation, he says before halting, as if about to divulge a deep secret, preparing his tongue to gratify all my needs at once. Yr delusion of mastery bears stains of my traumatic senselessness. Let me be yr tranquil erosion, the economy's vanishing causal force. Even after swallowing his piss, I still see myself everywhere I look, a series of seemingly endless grammatical subordinations, circling the withdrawn violence that structures the limits of our perceptual field, a blank in my own dislocation. It's a beautiful place and extends in every direction, said my soldier with no hands, and I imagine his fist up my ass. Elbow deep, I love the feeling, and quiver with pleasure at the thought of being so near the goal. A fragment of mobile space, truer than the whole that's false as the sun. This fantasy keeps my delusion far from what terminus over-codes all movement in advance. I, being where his blood's no longer flowing, or where the shipping lanes cross. There's a structure of hierarchies embedded in this feeling, a whole spectacle of surface becoming sentient, my functionalist metaphysics. An anarchy of symptoms soon emerges as a self-enclosed order of signs and I kiss the hole in his chest, anxious to feel some semblance of a self inside any cavity whatever.

Consonant with the rules of self-regulation, I keep turning over the same old ground. Just miswrote *police speech situation,* thinking about our language experiments, the way they succeed inside all the current contracts. There goes that stump again. Belongs to a man of action, a real mensch who'd cut the throat of a terrorist with box-cutters. The feel of his balls in my mouth is pretty hot, and his theory of agrarian development in the South is even hotter. Price packaging beefs up the social force of time. But one can hardly call this political literature, at least not in the real sense of the word political. At best, my lines draw on a few baked ideas and plot their paths sort of radial-like, tracing the movement of sugar and corn, raw cane imported from Hawaii, beets from the peninsula, recycled steel from China for ships, massive ships, big battle ships, hugest facility on the whole Pacific Rim. And while the good life would negate the conditions that make my poems possible, I still get off on high-performance synthetics, the body being this imaginary whole, like the space of property and money. From gantry cranes to scaffolding, just assault the system with hokum, coming on junk investments, dreaming of dressage. The way they burn the bodies, on certain days, when there's a gentle breeze coming from the north, what sweet odors move me. If y're quiet, you might hear the war moving thru every sound I make. Like his cremains, unidentifiable chips of bone ground to a fine powder for making the paste. It doesn't matter what you believe, this being the thing's one great achievement. There's a strong signal coming from a water hole just west of the great pacific garbage patch where the effluent of our consumption, draining with my humours deep in hollowed seascape, feeds back into fat. No common eye, the plastic gyre itself, so Archimedean, and from whose withdrawn point there emanates everything we can't perceive, the void in which it all hangs. Being is a value-slope, a residue of aura hardening inside refurbished Gulf War mat obstruction now used for detecting low flying drug smuggling planes and immigrant bodies crossing in the East, the way this memo moves, from foreskin to forethought, overstimulation falling prey to easy recognition.

Failing to arouse what can't be apprehended, wandering narrow corridors in search of better aid, my fancy turns on soldiers and migrant workers, whose terminus defines all movement in advance. Patches of heather here and there, thistle, columbine, and rag. Fondling these pared-down phrases, this report registers a breakdown in system-wide deference, another turn in the spiral of error, what these memoranda perpetuate. Slipping spirit into bone, a counterfeit resolve, the poem marks a starless place where nothing collides, my own body having become the scene of off-gassing and expelled energy where the grid bears down on every sound I'll never make. Singing thru a soldier's arms, I find myself mysteriously altered, unwilling to kill the gesture that might exceed what histories penetrate my form. After all the banks go down *what hardened shapes, what starry eyes* I lose the power to distinguish myself from those whom I referred to only a moment before as being indifferent to the generic malfeasance. Again, I ask, who can remain the context of one's own ecstasy. The writing betrays every effort, a severed limb, or rump. Returning thus transfigured to that scene, I induce alternate visions, eating trace particles, whatever precipitates in powders and gels along the wooded edge, barnacle encrusted borderland, where the vehicle stalls for an unknown period during which we wait to be subsumed by local controls, absorbed by the fluctuating value of timber and steel. Just crush the debris into a mealy paste until you become clear, yr body numinous, a phantom abandoned in a lifeless flow. Upon noticing fine spores colonizing the glass still moist with yr breath, I reach for baggie and tweezers and gather a specimen as if to contain the thing's triumphant reach, or capture my own capitulation. An otherwise smothered voice calls me thru the broken valves. Between equal rights, force decides. What surplus shatters every frame, it's even more devastating when feeling very far away, as this feeling of no feeling fails to correspond to any of the cataloged registers or moods. Afraid of this paralysis, I flee the purity of my own spasm, incorporated blank dissolve, pushing these figures of a self thru 63-grade ore, exquisite nonsite of my polis.

Clinging to my thesis goes on breeding these bad feelings. Ordered to release the prisoners, my soldier drags this beautiful guy to a nearby ditch and fucks him there instead. His body, a thing that penetrates my home. Don't turn on the light, he says, it's only real when the place is dark. Limbs frail, his veil wanting. But now he's dead, old calyx of my cauliflower, stem of the collard green. Stiff, unseen, toe-tagged, illegible script, the matter of consensus, casualty of every comfort for which his working-class youth had dreamed, being what my station denies. And so I've ceased pronouncing the name by which he'd once been hailed. Other impossible phonemes might make better contact with the future, as if that thing weren't in my mouth already, a memory hung upon yr body, the regulations by which it'll all one day be hanged. Nourished in yr wound, omission of the weakest link, something I no longer feel, upon which all I can feel depends. Bungling armed dilettante, a short-term capital management plan, value's been grafted to a soldier's stump, suffering in a limb where suffering will never take place. This is a picture of all the names gone missing. Subject to forestalling, engrossing, and regrating, occupied in feeble possession. Suppressing implications of analogy, oil spills like precious lube, the way money fills my rectum. Singing this inside the history of war songs, the sound of metal splits my hair, arousing the need for more credit. Migratory birds respond to similar disruptions, as they would some new tilting of the earth. Local flowers, forgotten in a soldier's hand where a thrust of my cock will never abolish chance. This one's got no skin, a name I've never heard, our stars, an endless slick. Reported language for all this being both true and false, like love we spread across foreclosed frontiers to an onsite container where the mere feel of precious metal, so many stately trodes connected to my balls, still goes a long way. There've been rumors of others shaken down for similar offence at the border, but the serious guys take one look at our powder blue wigs and wave us right on thru.

Being a belated effect of the war, my impotence opens like a void, filling this exquisite vacancy with nothing but itself. Thus the spirit's wiped clean, purged, leaving this residue of life, a hardened edge of mucous and bile. Like a film of cash, yr hot soldier jizz, never again on earth becoming. Hints of delicate squalor, whose concentration once hovered like a nimbus above the ones who go burning now. Wonder drapes his lower parts like a shroud. Their bodies fail to appear within our frame of reference, no material trace, no mark of any sort, nothing of the organ, tongue, or bone. *The fault is mine, impute it to me!* and so I scream into totality. Inside all the holding cells and johns, jerking-off to images of early modern plagues, both the waterborne and skin-to-skin, big dicks grown fat on all the multitudes and flows. Maybe this activity, more than some rote marshalling of pleasure, might transform, as if by voice alone, the stately currents and triumphal airs that make it hard to breathe inside places of great power, I mean the phone booths and the changing stalls. Being but a reflex in the instinct to preserve, becoming nothing but a thing to insert. Others reach for us from deep inside the world's once burnished fade. I can't soldier the way I used to, and this is taking a toll on my fantasies. My gunner baffles even the most astute of scientific minds. On nites like this, I can hear his voice still calling me naked to the window, as if to see the money changing hands. Drafting lists of pestilential fevers, my sickness grows tranquilly, rivaling the demands of other historical processes (shopping, fucking), atavistic tics by comparison and no refuge from the newfangled financial instruments. Some still say 'nickel and diming', pilfering scattered shreds of time, the working day, now irrelevant as a unit of measure, tho its command continues to penetrate my drift. Up to now, I've been slow to grasp the thing looming right before me, like his militarized form, or my empty reflection in the word it stands for. Having negated the injunction to negate the need to work, we've been plied with demands for more flexible figures, in whose fantasy resentment bogs, a soiled calculation, festering swan-like in the fashionable disdain for song.

Pronounced dead, a soldier becomes my disappearing act. The consistency of the situation hangs on the body, being a hole around which everything that appears appears to cohere. It's a spell that holds me in thrall, unable to distinguish my proper subject from one deceased. Being what the language doesn't want me to do, the decision to autopsy all US war casualties helps the military eliminate equipment flaws by improving a fleet of crash test dummies. Whatever words exist for this fall apart at such a stunning rate as if to protect the value of each identity, parceling properties before they sell. Caving to these demands, I masturbate to fantasies of day laborers fucking me in the shadow of the screening station, a checkpoint beside the border's river diversion system where they're reinforcing old security fence before it can deform under a migrant's weight. I can't get hard enough for intercourse when the moment is sweet, but as soon as he asserts the fundamental right to liberty and happiness, being what my soldier has sworn to protect, I fall on my knees, take his member in my mouth and beg him to discharge. Whatever shame I feel in the face of sovereignty is inseparable from this arousal. In a world of love and domination, sex becomes monstrous in just proportion to the monstrosity of that world. The skin, being this endless organ of excitement and abuse, my own private pleasures being mere adjunct of that. Don't confuse this sentence for a proposition. Time itself, having already become a hardened artifact of the system, renders my orgasm co-extensive with the demands of production, but this is neither true nor false.

In other words, time is a fighter jet, the way the spirit is a bone, and the object of my rage secretes the same auratic halo. Like the best philosopher, my soldier subtracts the real from what can be thought and this enhances his allure, makes me love him even more. Translated into military language, the point is not to shoot, but to clarify the shot. So precision bombing has penetrated my poems and yet not even a single one of my feelings is precise, the words even less so. Put another way, the self is a coin. And while a soldier's corpse may be the limit of my world, his cock in my ass remains a vehicle of transport, the light by which I write this sentence, whose sense defies the stars.

O B S C E N E
I N T I M A C I E S

— nowhere to lay the body that isn't here —

•

Against this backdrop of total
- ity figures having found re
- lief as I have in my bowels

So bloated with event who
Walks away from it as I do
Having walked away from

Theater the barnyard filth
And debris lodged down de
- ep in soft tissue his severed

Genitals flown wider still
Shored against ruin gaps we
- deged or driven into being

        — there being no deep inside spectacle.

•

My soldier died last September hit
By Taliban mortar while trying to fix
A tank tread his father feeling the boy

Had been murdered by insurgents
Wanted to see the post-mortem report
To verify other accounts he heard a

- bout the 24-year-old's death so o
- ffer comfort I say to myself say
The reservist died instantly when a

Hot piece of shrapnel tore thru the boy
- 's flak vest into his chest before break
- ing in 2 w/ 1 piece lodged in the left

Aorta leaving the other piece lodged
In left lung a mute & uncomplaining
Sleep being fatal form his figure

                    — *my decaying dream.*

●

At the time of the incident weather conditions
In Oruzgan were very bad with rain low clouds
Large dust storms seriously reducing visibility

An army spokesperson said the event occurred
In an area where military efforts need boosting
As we continue to expand our influence Tangy

Valley is one area we need to get into the unit
Looking hard for improvised explosive devices
But they may not have been specifically looking

For them as part of the mission that day tho soldiers
Had successfully discovered several insurgent caches
Including large amounts of explosives despite small

But significant successes it has been a difficult
Dangerous mission for the boys they've lost one
Of their mates and need to know they are inside

Our thoughts as they look after each other do
Important work particularly when they grievc
No doubt our bonds will be

                    — *strengthened by this loss.*

•

One soldier returned in a state of decom
- position so severe that viewing his body
Was impossible only 3 days after his death

Being bio-ruin's outer ring what horizon
Whose sensation my rim a negative imprint
The world image collateralized risk mech

- anism a current military procedure to pack
Fallen soldiers in ice then transport them
To US Air Force Base for a 3 step process

1) Identification which includes DNA dental
& fingerprinting, 2) Autopsy and 3) Preparation
I.e. embalming the body a proper mortuary

Facility were one only in place over there
We'd have been able to say our goodbyes
But the boy was not

                    — *even refrigerated.*

•

The body appears to have been
Dead some time under a spell a
Dream nation water hood flex

- cuffs minor abrasions sub
- galeal hemorrhage bilateral
Frontal regions of scalp intra

- muscular hemorrhage of an
- terior aspect & nothing internal
Evidence of trauma scant

Cause of death indeterminate
Toxicology report negative
For alcohol and drugs I long

—for where yr pleasure lies.

•

After spending weeks studying the autopsy re ˉ
- port of a handsome soldier killed in Iraq it be
- comes clear he'd been tortured by his captors

Some say they held him for up to four months
And those four months must have been hell the
Boy's stepfather told the San Antonio Express

News for its Sunday edition when the autopsy
Results arrived a month ago there were words
Of caution like I strongly recommend you read

This in the presence of people who can provide
You with emotional support during this time such
As yr minister a family friend or a counselor

The office of the Armed Forces Medical Examiner
Wrote in a cover letter and someone read parts
Of the report aloud omitting graphic details trying

To shelter the mother from them *I've mourned*
I've cried it isn't known how the boy was treated
Before he died severe decomposition of his

Remains make it difficult to reach conclusions
But the one-page autopsy report and its four-page
Supplement offer clues that my soldier may

Have been beaten and dismembered before he
Was killed and buried in a shallow grave the report
- 's last page says the nose had been broken but had

Well healed prior to death and the report also de
- scribes foot bones detached from commingled re
- mains fingers wrapped in a blanket part of a hand

- cuff was found remains had decayed & demon
- strated substantial sun-bleaching after being dug up
Partly eaten by animals during the night

                    — *time in which suns perish.*

●

One young man detained by US authorities died
As a result of asphyxia lack of oxygen to the brain
From strangulation evidenced by a fractured hyoid

Bone in the neck & soft tissue hemorrhage
Extending downward to the level of the right
Thyroid cartilage a heart grown cold & bursting

Contusions in mid abdomen along spine and but
- tocks extending to the left flank abrasions
On lateral buttock abrasions on back of legs

Knees contusions left wrist lacerations & super
- ficial cuts on right 4th and 5th fingers missing
Blunt force injuries testes swollen purple pre

- dominantly recent contusions blue on torso
Lower back and extremities abrasions red
Consistent with use of restraints no evidence

Of defense no injuries no natural disease cause
Of death has been determined to be homicide
With his mission fulfilled this one had nothing

       — *and with nothing more to give, I learn to love you still.*

•

An odd isolated shrapnel wound it unfortunate
- ly implicated a critical area & caused his death
Which is particularly troubling because it's terrible

A stroke of fate to have that happen a major
Cause of fatalities being broken spines inflicted
When an armored vehicle is struck by a bomb

Blast it's like being hurled about inside I mean
It's like you take an egg & put it in this metal box

— now shake the metal box around.

•

A signature wound on our heroic troops
In Kabul where most soldiers have been
Diagnosed with traumatic brain injury

Or TBI caused by the impact of IEDs
As the explosions keep getting bigger aid
Stations may be capable of stabilizing it

But aren't equipped to treat TBI so all
We can do is assess it treat its signs
Symptoms an invisible wound a world

The army uses techniques like MACE
Military Acute Concussion Exam to find
Confessions whiplash memory loss seve

- re headaches altho it's terribly hard
To know sometimes but the soldiers them
- selves are the best tools since they do ob

- serve each other they know how one
Behaves when not being normal but I
Will never know

                    — *what you really are.*

•

A young man was found unresponsive restrained
In his cell death being due to blunt force injuries
To lower extremities complicating coronary artery

Disease contusions & abrasions on forehead
Nose head behind ear neck abdomen buttock
Elbow thigh knee foot toe w/ hemorrhage

On rib area & leg blunt force injuries resulted
In extensive muscle damage muscle necrosis &
Rhabdomyolysis electrolyte disturbances primarily

Hyperkalemia elevated blood potassium level &
Metabolic acidosis occurs within hours of muscle
Damage massive sodium and water shifts occur re

- sulting in hypovolemic shock & casodilatation
And later acute renal failure the deceased's un
- derlying coronary artery disease would compromise

Ability to tolerate electrolyte & fluid abnormalities
Underlying malnutrition so it's likely dehydration
Only exacerbated the effects of muscle damage

Mere bones of desolation now things

— *my love restores.*

•

An autopsy on another boy alleged
To have been killed by a US Marine
And five other servicemen revealed

He was probably not bound by hands
& feet as the government reported
But likely rather *murthered* meaning

Smothered in the midst of camp a wel
- come gift severe decay makes learning
All the facts impossible and the army won't

Reveal details of autopsy but a spokes
- person sings of a body badly decom
- posed nature's naked loveliness buried

Then exhumed for examination a heart
Made callous by many blows

— *composed of my most penetrable stuff.*

•

Then my soldier changed his gait his voice
Deepened he acted manly tho it was all pretty
Strange I mean here's a boy who told them

He was quite a gay boy at 16 after escaping
The fists of football players when hockey
Players came to his rescue and his car

Was spray painted *Go Home Fag!* at 29
He told them of his life how it was missing
Camaraderie brotherhood I'm joining

The army he said a composer a peace act
- ivist a math genius studied palindromes
maps patterns the US Constitution quantum

Physics the army had never really crossed
The mind of his left-leaning parents googling
Kandahar his father tracked every soldier

Killed in the far-off land and then at the same
Oak table where the boy said he was joining
Up they learned he was gone O soldier

Of infectious smile I have maintained bachelor
Status with the strictest of discipline he wrote
A discipline I secretly wish would be compro

- mised by a charming beauty he wrote that too
Never used gay or homosexual to define himself
Being the least interesting thing about this one

Who earned the nickname Slovak for his macho
His exaggerated arrow-straight gait a ham who
Found a way to fit in when he laughed he threw

His head back closed his eyes released moans
Made everyone else chuckle in combat he rode
With an African-American one from Hawaii

And a Latino they were like Team Minority
But intelligent don't begin to describe him I
Mean I feel smarter when I kiss his organ a

- orta lung stomach finding meaning in organs
We bonded at boot camp ligaments and con
- nective tissue being fragile like brothers

The only difference being going to war no
Topic taboo we shared everything how hard
It can be being queer in America and a soldier

En route to guard duty at the tower one day
In a Kandahar police station reading *Time*
About gay teens who commit suicide after

Being bullied a massive bomb lay hidden a mor
- tar round along the route detonated beneath
Him children scattered three other explosives

Daisy-chained failed to get off and I imagine
Myself 20 meters ahead of my battle buddy
Whose legs were blown off as was his left hand

Delivered severe wounds to his head there
Being a different kind of gravity at the edge
The universe an autopsy report on the table

Maybe I'd have been killed too I think had the o
- thers exploded maybe I'd have rushed to his side
Within seconds a medic joined a terrible training

Session but it was all too real to sanitize the info
Described for accuracy physical
Details of remains

> — *the hair I cherish in a box.*

•

My vision being a soldier's body found
In the brush of an extremely rough area
A training region near the land navigation

Course the terrain covered with trees
Brush area temperatures in the mid
To low 90s when the boy went missing

In a place heavily laden with creeks &
Drinkable water tho it remains unclear
Whether this one had any water with him

And when his body's found rose-robed
In dazzling immortality it's unclear how
How long he had been dead there being

No sign no indication of any attack it is
Devastating to lose any soldier but this
One was a model soldier always looking

For the next task to complete his last
Status update *gone for 2 weeks so hit me*
Up later! before the body turns belly

Up in the rising sun

          — my sunk extinct refulgent prime.

•

The boy was vulnerable captured
By Navy Seal Team #7 he resisted
Apprehension external injuries in

- cluding multiple contusions con
- sistent w/ injuries sustained during
Detention fractures of the ribs

Puncture of the left lung imply
Significant blunt force injuries of
Thorax likely resulted in impaired

Respiration ligature marks of wrists
Ankles remote gunshot wound to torso
With no significant natural diseases

Identified according to investigating
Agents an interrogation hood made
Of synthetic material had been placed

Over the head and neck white faced
And still such beauty

— *in which all things work and move.*

•

And then another soldier died in cus
- tody blunt force trauma & choking gag
- ged in standing restraint cause of death

Swollen purple and asphyxia auto
- psy reveals deep bruising of the chest
Wall numerous displaced rib fractures

Bruising on the lungs hemorrhage in
- to the mesentery of the small and large
Intestine the neck structures reveal

Hemorrhage into the strap muscles
And fractures of the thyroid cartilage
And hyoid bone history being of

Asphyxia secondary to occlusion of
The oral airway pleural and pulmonary
Adhesions hypertensive cardiovascular

Disease according to reports provided
By the US army shackled to the top
Of a doorframe with a gag in his mouth

At the time he lost consciousness be
- came pulseless the severe blunt force
Injuries the hanging position & ob

- struction of the oral cavity with a gag
Contributed to his death

                    — *being one with commerce.*

•

Sometimes the remains arrive at the mil
- itary morgue intact sealed inside a human
Remains pouch or body bag & other times

They arrive as dissociated remains i.e. a leg
An arm finger lobe bone shard tooth even
Eyes ears or other body parts ripped loose

By the force of a roadside device a suicide
Bomber or air crash sometimes there are
Commingled remains of several victims

Of a blast or ambush including service work
- ers & civilian bystanders the most common
Cause of death in this war is neither bullet

Infection nor cholera but rather homemade ex
- plosives and execution-style killings autopsies
DNA fingerprints tissue analysis and pain

- staking observation help make positive id
- entifications it being a noble mission to un
- ravel mysteries borne of war to provide

Families of the fallen with the full truth
About a death to know the remains survivors
Receive belong to their loved ones

                — *and to no one else.*

•

O leprous corpse monster of life
- 's waste killing suns for time
Being nothing left to see show

Me the secrets of matter & why
Yr blood's not my blood yr shit
My shit expelled into the same

Void & why yr cells yr tears are
Not my cells my tears contract
- ing nothing concrete wounds

Being nothing but this language
For a soldier's rush toward the real
- ization of uselessness

— sire of our common strain.

•

Material drawn from site reports: Al Asad, Iraq (1/9/2004); Bagram Theater Internment Facility, Bagram, Afghanistan (12/10/2002); Whitehorse Detainment Facility, Nasiriyah, Iraq (6/6/2003). Additional material drawn from an Operation Iraqi Freedom investigation initiated upon notification by Combat Support Hospital Mortuary Affairs Office, having identified two US soldiers killed following an ambush. Original exhibits remain classified and retained in files of Combat Support Hospital, Fort Bliss TX 79906. Other classified exhibits retained in files of staff Judge Advocates Office, 81ˢᵗ BCT, Camp Murray WA 98430. Originals of additional exhibits used also classified and retained in files of Armed Forces Institute of Pathology. Originals of still further exhibits used retained in files of the US Army Criminal Investigation Laboratory, N. 2ⁿᵈ St., Forest Park GA. Originals of final exhibit retained in evidence depository, Camp Victory, Iraq, APO AE 09342. Also used: available military intelligence and witness interviews, as well as "Soldier leaves legacy much larger than 'he was gay,'" CNN (7/2/2011), and "Soldiers' Brain Injuries from Blasts in Afghanistan Take a Toll," New York Daily News (9/20/2009). Other sources include Percy Bysshe Shelley's "Adonais" and Walt Whitman's *Drum-Taps*.

WHITHER PORN?, OR THE SOLDIER AS ALLEGORY

— away from self-expression but not from personal life —

The million animiculae that graze upon this planet
were created and endowed with organs and sense
solely to enable them to contemplate the soldier.
Charles Baudelaire, "Some French Caricaturists"

I've been told it can take years before one is able to grasp what one has written. I still don't understand a book I wrote called *Rumored Place*, so unresolved and in flight from itself. That work concludes with a blank or a bar [——] *placeholder for all we can't perceive haunting all we can* like the mark of something withdrawn from sense, which had migrated thru my book, a floating caesura separating visible and invisible *logic of porn* audible and inaudible *aesthetic of state secrets*. *Music for Porn* emerged rather feebly in that blank as my writing began to seek the shape of what could not be felt there, the content of that form like the plenitude of a void.

The poems whose music issues from this fault in perception *constant interruption* were seeking *groping* a figure, any shape or hieroglyph that might animate the contradictions *near perfect correspondence* between personal life and the regimes of representation *property and selfhood* that mediate my intimacies, be it to the bodies I love or the countless others withdrawn in scenes of conflict and catastrophe and to which my body is joined thru flows of arms and money, bodies I'll never see but whose lack of being *over there* has been contracted to my well-being here.

The soldier keeps repeating myself. Disjoined from the world of values whose extension he is, he appears in blank erotic haze. Like an emanation, he emerges in a fault running thru militarized common sense *extension of my body* which he so spectacularly realizes. His appearance and reappearance won't quit, like a skip or a tic *symptomatic spasm I can finally feel* a figure I am only able to contemplate now *as if for the first time* and whose seeming centrality to my book is a consequence of this slow accretion of sensation, not its reason. In other words, the soldier is a phantom synthesis *artifice, fake* a cause summoned by its own effects. Check out how I fuse my attention to his form *this fault in judgment* as if his form had been present from the work's inception. But the soldier is not a concept, certainly not an original one, tho he may be an allegory *mirror of ideology, from which there's no remove* a blank that both arouses and frustrates my longing for a livable world, at once portal and obstruction.

It's in the fault where I first encounter my apparition. The soldier appears at a remote sentry near the river, dripping wet, shivering, and clad in nothing but his headgear. [1] He appears shaken, the light of worlds in his eyes, genuine in every way, tho still able to walk it off. The soldier appears confused, if not demented, while bearing in his arms my own half-dressed and lifeless form. He appears to have been shot by security forces, his head shaven and with a slight beard, wearing traditional gray, loose fitting Afghan salwar kameez clothing. Dressed up in an orange jumper and green anorak, the soldier appears with his hands tied, legs spread eagle. He appears to have been trussed, but he's helpful at first, his limbs sun burnt and mighty, his thighs like great military engines capable of wielding the heavy weapons themselves. Like a comic strip character, the soldier appears and reappears, again and again, his features amplified and distorted like those of the capitalist, the worker, the terrorist, his head shaven, with a slight beard, wearing nothing at all but a bit of traditional loose fitting camouflage, his particularity being no more than a type, unclad and yielding, nothing but his headgear, lasers coming from his eyes, sublime music from his core. Despite being held at gunpoint with his hands tied, trussed and moaning, he appears to be healthy, no trace of the fabled powders in his stool. He can barely contain my rage, his fear, this love. He has a hard time remaining erect, and no longer comes at all. Again and again, he appears and reappears, shaken, capable, genuine, confused, sun burnt and mighty thighs, generator of magnificent light in which I find myself distracted, my head buried in his crotch, or his in mine, a sentence from which we might never emerge. He appears to sense me in a similar state and, even tho I'm now lodged in a safe house down the road, far from the current unrest, I've been made pregnant with his child. There's no evidence at all, nothing but a feeling in a limb I can't locate, an organ I can't name, but the soldier appears to want me, or rather, he appears to sense how we're both in the same condition, taken aboard the same flight, and I immediately love him for this reflection of my hollow impression, love him as myself, a song I can't sing without singing his. [2]

As my poems begin to stir in the fault, the blank [——] recedes and in its place there emerges this phony apparition *fragile appearance* which seems to sense *materialize* a fundamental convergence *interpenetration* of private intimacies and public attitudes *pleasure and surveillance, affection and war*. Value clings to the soldier like self-preservation *a film of cash, relation of no relation* betraying my love for the death drive. This is how history succumbs to natural force, which erodes its stable meanings with implacable puissance as they incline toward ruin and waste. My soldier is no match for this, he's too real, being capital's proper corpus, extension of its management and concern. Still the soldier has a hard time not exposing himself *his member* as caricature or parody. As if to parry history's blow, he appears like an allegory of contemporary decay, dislodging word from meaning, driving a wedge between costume and life, subjecting even the most reliable of all appearances *his own* to the dissipation it is his function to forestall. This is how a transparent appearance *all buxom mass and sterling girth* becomes my gross opacity.

But my soldier, he's allegorical by default because whatever language there might be to denote his corpse does not exist in the public sphere, so there's no other way to sustain a relation with that phantom synthesis over time. Appearance and value are rent asunder in his beauty *this chasm in sense, an emptiness that's killing me*. Having cut himself loose from the social relations that make him what he is, his figure stands in for universal profit. His body, my dissipative structure, a temporary life form, or species of provisional order *like a poem* conditioned by a state of ever increasing disorder, but whose ephemeral aura assumes the function of something secure, something constant, something fixed. Sensing its own decay, value clings with fierce tenacity to the very things *bodies* that will be sacrificed for it. Just as he disavows the debauchery of capital *whose servant he is* my soldier becomes evermore debauched *sinks below the hemisphere of sense, as I might sink my nose in his ass* down along the precipitous fault of old imperialisms. With the militarization *financialization* of daily life, lyric is caught up in these same abstractions *value credit debt* as overproduction penetrates the soldier's body and weds it strangely to my own *radical discontinuity of flesh and world that the poem longs to bridge.*

Working overtime as allegory, the soldier's body *hieroglyph of value* can enter my poems because its representation has been severed from the real bodies of military men. And so, the Soldier appears, an exaggerated type like one you'd see in gay porn from the 70s when the artifice of narrative and the masque of character were still important for arousing pleasure. Or, he might appear among the Village People, that band of iconic queer bodies: Indian Chief, Construction Worker, Leatherman, Cowboy, Cop, Soldier. His figure occupies a place in the social imaginary tho its relation to me has been entirely mystified, stimulating desire while blocking any living tie to the bodies his figure represents *occults* except insofar as that tie already binds me. All these relations saturate my poems' form, which alone allows me to feel them, to arouse and mobilize them against the mirror play of dead things.

Hazy eros *residue of money* hovers around this figure, and settles on my skin. I can't wash myself of its thick condensation and my poems have lost that apotropaic power to deflect the soldier's image, to keep it from usurping my own whenever I gaze in the mirror. The poems want to feel something *buried improvised device* to destroy this reflection, anything to activate whatever improvisation will have to have occurred here in order for tomorrow to be other than today, a future that fails to resemble the ongoing accumulation and privation that constitute the present. As part of an effort to ensure its claim on false futurity *extension of dead time* the present resurrects a fantasy of meaning *identity* that animates the soldier's figure like a ghost *money*. No doubt, Melville senses this in "A Utilitarian View of the Monitor's Flight" when he identifies the modern soldier *circa 1862* as mere "operative," incarnation of the hoary warrior, who, in yet another manifestation *today* will become a prosthetic of finance, a tomb of meaning *never there to begin with* as it becomes one with nature.

And just as nature abrades the stone, history abrades *revolts* its most constant forms, denying them of all but the most transient meaning, revealing the transitory bent *hallucination* of historical significance. At the same time, history, like allegory, formalizes the erosion of its own meanings, generating signs for that which bears no visible signs. This is how capital organizes the imperceptible relations that make our life-world a function of the abstract and fungible *infinite exchange of bodies and things* identifying the human corpus as but another limit to move beyond, "to dump your gorgeous body, now deceased / where the other garbage goes." [3]

For Baudelaire, all human forms *body, statue, corpse* become haunted with the hemorrhaged life that usurps them *money, commodity, war*. Written during the same period as Whitman's *Leaves of Grass*, Baudelaire's *Les Fleurs du mal* offers an organic allegory for becoming inorganic. Attuned to the naturalization of capital, Baudelaire praises degraded things in a language of natural sensation. "The soldier has his beauty, just as the prostitute and the dandy have theirs," he writes in "The Painter of Modern Life." Anticipating how we've materialized our own dematerialization, his poems return the body to "a throng of wandering lost desires," which have themselves become allegories *zombies of living labor*. And whereas Whitman consolidates an emblem of restored fraternal order *national unity* in the figure of the fallen soldier, Baudelaire loses himself, subliming the perfection of a soldier's toilet, his immaculate dress and cosmetic comportment. Here he might find a pleasure comparable to the spectacle of a setting sun, "a headless corpse emitting a stream of blood" *dizzying array of poignant splendors, cascade of molten metal, paradise of fire, dazzling colonnades* hieroglyph of militarized common sense.

My soldier thus becomes my swan, my muse, my washed-up whore. Like an allegory, he hardens around all our abstract relations *values* assuming a shape around history's contusions and contradictions, a scar where my alienable form has been hygienically sutured to the loss he represents. Referring to something with which it no longer coincides *the signs that bloat his corpse* my apparition appears *by disappearing* while the soldier manifests a void *absence of what he stands for.* What would it feel like to rematerialize his body as my own *fate of all our proprietary claims* as if this hasn't already occurred? His body entombs *sustains* the absence of its own referent, and so my soldier is a terminal melancholic *or is that me.* A studied nihilist, he incorporates an order of transcendent meaning *democracy, freedom, trade* while the ground of such meaning becomes the ground of our catastrophe. My soldier is the narrative of these disjunctions *story of identity with nothing inside* eternal integument *hardened skin* around a liquidated meaning, as if his hardening alone could arrest these processes of decay.

Adjunct of multimillion dollar contracts, my soldier appears within an apparatus of control *pornography, prosthetic of police* where the visible and the invisible, funded and defunded, normal and pathological, public and private, militant and military, impersonal and intimate are produced, delimited, and reinforced. But porn is so ambivalent, it can always go both ways. Without denoting an essential quality of the image, porn connotes a whole technology for governing the tension between eros and identity, life and death. Porn brings to light, permits, and publicizes, just as it darkens, prohibits, and privatizes. Check out all the closed and repetitive codes *privileging male pleasure* ensuring hierarchies and machines of domination. Like the military, pornography is a biopolitical operation for regulating the social body and all the particular bodies that comprise it, admitting some, canceling others. Under such regimes, common sense itself becomes a kind of pornography *expropriation of my most intimate relations* just as pornography becomes a kind of common sense *everything bearing visible value, everything erasing the relations that produce it.* So one must speak in the pornographic even as one speaks against it, or rather against the ends to which it's been yoked *to overturn common sense from within common sense itself* and this informs my poems' frustrated and obsessive arousal.

As apocalypse *revelation* of the canceled body, pornography alternately becomes a tactic for undermining those same hierarchies and machines, introducing inassimilable bodies and pleasures into orders of invisibility and surveillance. Disabling self-enclosed delusions of sovereignty, porn *prophylactic against the soldier's hygiene* disturbs the very divisions it erects, potentiating new bodies that render the old corrupt. A bleeding guy in uniform *wounded boy in an Afghan village* fallen guarantor of America's future: these images arouse me. They touch my nerves and stir my senses before the affects they stimulate *excitement rage shame* can be properly channeled. Whatever these feelings, I want them to exceed my frame *to arrive at a large and public intimacy* as the intimate and abstract persist in and thru each other. And so, while porn could be any order of representation *sex, war, money* whereby our most sensual relations are mediated, organized, and policed by technologies of the image *distillations of capital laminated to my skin* entangling my most personal relations with the most impersonal processes, porn has an equal and opposite potential to challenge, disturb, and transform these fragile organizations of visibility.

Soldiers, sex, and money: things toward which an allegorical imagination inclines as it grasps a form wherein a plenitude of meaning *value* coincides with its own liquidation. Nature hardens in the money form *whore's make-up, soldier's thighs*. Appendage of finance *most allegorical of capital's regimes* the soldier assumes a place beside that of the prostitute in whose body intimacy and commerce exist for each other. Vehicle of exchange and pleasure *receptacle of cash and cum* the soldier's physique arouses and neutralizes the relation between money and life, just as he eroticizes technologies of control. Constructed by money for the protection of money *social relation as death* he lacks the very thing for which his figure has been assembled. His sold hole bears the stain of my overproduction. In other words, my social alienation may be completed in the body of a soldier, and so in loving him I can finally love myself.

Today, the US soldier's body becomes a perfect pornograph when its a dead body *casualty of finance, guarantor of my pleasure* a body whose image has been legally withheld, removed from public circulation, just as its autopsy report has been classified in order to preserve the values that body died for, values transfigured in the soldier whose hard muscle materializes our common resource, first rendered as sacrifice *purity of waste* and then withdrawn from view.

[——].

Music for Porn issues in the scene of this withdrawal.

1 // *Bully for Brontosaurus* by Stephen Jay Gould.

2 // *Anomalies and Curiosities of Medicine*, written in 1896 by physicians George M. Gould and Walter L. Pyle, tells the story of a soldier wounded during a Civil War battle. "The fighting was fierce, hope was slim and a split second after our soldier was shot, a piercing cry was heard in a house near the battleground, but remote enough to have warranted the expectation of safe protection. Examination of the wounded soldier showed that a bullet had passed through the scrotum and carried away the left testicle. The same 'minie bal' with some spermatozoa upon it had apparently penetrated the left side of a woman's abdomen midway between the umbilicus and the anterior of the ileum, and become lost in the abdomen. She suffered an attack of peritonitis. Two hundred and seventy-eight days after the reception of the ball, she was delivered of a fine boy, weighing eight pounds, to the surprise of herself and the mortification of her parents."

3 // Baudelaire, "Burial" in *Les Fleurs du mal*. A similar image turns up in Jean Genet's *Funeral Rites*: "Nothing prevented me from seeing in the garbage can the momentary and marvelous figure." The figure here is the body of Genet's lover, who died on the barricades. Genet's incredible conceits constantly transfigure the body of his dead soldier into the most incommensurate things, from a Venetian flask to a sausage feeding the city of Paris.

DEDICATION

after Emerson

Coming down from sublime heights, now speaking more directly, and with compassion for our defenders, all these jottings assume some part in the war. Sporadic anecdotes, surrounding vast tracts of nature, there's no monopoly on frivolous violation. Slabs dug, discs laid, an obelisk rises in the square, my rare and solitary growth, an altar where noble youth, delicately brought up, will come to make their secret vows. What eloquent inscriptions the shaft now bears. There's a great deal that is personal and local here, tho I'm having trouble remembering this. Common country, noble names. Bearing no reference to utility, the dead borrow six words at a time. No doubt, I delight to record, and I guess we're all well aware of the facts, whatever dumb sense assures. War civilizes. Being our unphilosophical pulse, integrity incorruptible, a glowing mass, my white heat, I mean, pure wizened heart, a throbbing universe, the chord that keeps the nation united binds us to our kindred, as we cling affectionately to houses, and others just as rich wrenched away from families and chores. For every principle a war-note burns as hotly. What delusions of brave men, a duty so severe, walking 80 miles thru the mud with nothing but liver, blackberries, and pennyroyal tea. The good of the day, like the moral qualities of a commander, spills on all my savings. Hush now and hear the sound of funeral echoes. How these dumb stones speak, how the shaft reveals whose manly beauty all of us remember as it discharges such immense results. Despite the annoyance of artillery fire, we hear more beautiful benedictions. Opposition being against the nature of things, the storm of war works a miracle on men. Sleeping with them all the time, tho threatened by their sickness, pitching quoits, looking rather ashamed, my military discipline, a sham-fight. Whatever the proverbial timidity of trade conceals, the war discovers. Even the secret architecture of things begins to disclose itself with no reference to utility. The incongruous militia burns, tender as a woman. This material force, the butchery and babes, a rally of all the manhood in the land, this war-blast makes meat of all our little bank accounts, every last resource, the old cow, my heifer, ten thousand letters, a solid mass, the rains and mud. All this talk of inactivity, of bull-dog fighting, grave, but social, a formal surrender, not for money, rather these necessities, what virtues can be sold. Armies, being nothing more than wandering cities, generate a vast heat and lift the burning spirit of my republic. Fair, blonde, the rose hangs long on his chest, his cheek, having laid him in two double blankets, the best box we could. Gone from the hearthstone, our courage too discharged, lifting sacrifice, the formal surrender, no badge or reminder, our gloom being nowhere near an end, tho our love, unequal to the charge, dispels it.

c

ACKNOWLEDGMENTS

Thank you to the editors of the following publications for instigating and supporting this work: *Damn the Ceasars, Sous les Pavés, The Swan's Rag, Chicago Review, Gam, Submodern Fiction, EOAGH, Crayon, Little Red Leaves, West Wind Review, Aufgabe, Joyland, Cambridge Literary Review, Wheelhouse,* and *Try!*. "Some Speculations Around George Oppen's Parousia" was first published in its entirety in *P-Queue*, generously attended to by Andrew Rippeon; and the initial poem of this same sequence appeared as a letterpress broadside, thanks to the work of Michael Cross whose guidance has been crucial to the making of this book. "This Evolve" was written for Elliot Anderson's artist's book of webcam photographs, *CAMS*. "Imaginary Politics" saw the light of day as a fine artisan chapbook by Tap Root Editions, for which inexpressible gratitude goes to bookmaker Blake Riley. Many thanks to Joel Kuszai and Factory School for critical support early on in the life of this project. Stephen Motika's belief in these pages and his vision at Nightboat Books allowed *Music for Porn* to find its final form.

Many of these pieces were written expressly for friends, without whom this work would not be what it is: "My Operatives," for Taylor Brady; "So Brave a Beginning as This," for Marc Schachter; "Armies of the Wounded," for Jocelyn Saidenberg; "Dedication," for C.J. Martin and Julia Drescher; "Remains Unwritten," for Thom Donovan. "Some Speculations" was written for Andrew Rippeon, John Wilkinson, Myung Mi Kim, Rachel Blau DuPlessis, Stephen Cope, Susan Thackrey and Thom Donovan, on the occasion of the Oppen Centenary at University of Buffalo.

Section epigraphs are adapted or quoted from the following sources: (1) *Rumored Place*; (2) George Oppen, Daybooks; (3) Walter Lowenfels, *Walt*

Whitman's Civil War; (4) unattributed, *Runaway Street Punk*, Gay Times Book Club; (5) Federico Garcia Lorca, "Casida of the Boy Wounded by the Water"; (6) Bhanu Kapil, conversation; (7) Kathy Acker, *The Childlike Life of the Black Tarantula by the Black Tarantula*. "Dedication" was written after Ralph Waldo Emerson's "Dedication of the Soldiers' Monument" (1867). The first line of "Some Speculations" quotes Oppen's "That Land," from "Five Poems About Poetry."

Music for Porn is dedicated to Lee Azus whose love and companionship exceed measure.

ISBN: 978-0-9844598-9-6

Design and typesetting by HR Hegnauer
Text set in Adobe Caslon Pro
Cover: "Untitled porn collage," by Tanya Hollis and Rob Halpern (2011)

Cataloging-in-publication data is available
From the Library of Congress

Distributed by University Press of New England
One Court Street
Lebanon, NH 03766
www.upne.com

Nightboat Books
Callicoon, New York
www.nightboat.org

NIGHTBOAT BOOKS

Nightboat Books, a nonprofit organization, seeks to develop audiences for writers whose work resists convention and transcends boundaries. We publish books rich with poignancy, intelligence, and risk. Please visit our website, www.nightboat.org, to learn about our titles and how you can support our future publications.

This book was made possible by a grant from the Topanga Fund, which is dedicated to promoting the arts and literature of California.

The following individuals have supported the publication of this book. We thank them for their generosity and commitment to the mission of Nightboat Books:

Elizabeth Motika
Benjamin Taylor

This book has been made possible, in part, by a grant from the New York State Council on the Arts Literature Program.

State of the Arts

NYSCA